TEARS FOR TARSHIHA

TEARS FOR TARSHIHA

OLFAT MAHMOUD

with Dani Cooper and Helen McCue

WILD DINGO PRESS

Published by Wild Dingo Press
Melbourne, Australia
books@wilddingopress.com.au
www.wilddingopress.com.au

First published by Wild Dingo Press 2018

Designer: Debra Billson
Editor: Catherine Lewis
Cover photos: Government Press Office (Israel);
Old Palestinian Tatreez-Embroidery Image: lenazap (iStock)
Print in Australia by Griffin Press

Mahmoud, Olfat, 1960.
Tears for Tarshiha / Olfat Mahmoud.

 A catalogue record for this
book is available from the
National Library of Australia

ISBN: 9780648066361 (paperback)
ISBN: 9780987178596 (ebook: pdf)
ISBN: 9780987381347 (eBook: ePub)

To my parents who nurtured in me my love of Palestine and
Tarshiha and my desire to return to my homeland.

ACKNOWLEDGEMENTS

For several decades my friends, in particular Helen McCue, my family and colleagues have been urging me to tell the story of my life as a child, teenager, wife, mother and activist living in the Palestinian refugee camp of Burj Barajneh in Beirut, Lebanon. It has taken time, but with the help of all these people *Tears for Tarshiha* has now been published.

I wish to acknowledge the gifts given to me by my parents and the love and encouragement given by my father and my mother who supported me throughout their lives. This book and all the work that I do would not have been possible without the love and support of my extended family, especially my husband Mahmoud and our boys, Chaker, Fayez, Hadi and Hani.

I am exceptionally grateful for the professional help in bringing my story to a wider audience from publisher Wild Dingo Press, and in particular its founder Catherine Lewis, who has an enduring commitment to giving voice to the world's refugees.

I am grateful to all the wonderful women, my sisters in the struggle, who have been through so much with me and have always been so loving and supportive. I acknowledge all of the international development agency staff, in particular Union Aid Abroad APHEDA, who have supported my work in the camps, and all the wonderful volunteers who have given their time and energy to help us. I would like to thank also the Oral History department of the National Library of Australia.

There have been a number of wonderful people who have read this manuscript and who have encouraged me to continue during the difficult times. Their sage advice and suggestions are the backbone on which this manuscript has been crafted. They know who they are without being named.

Finally, I wish to thank Dani Cooper and Helen McCue for their encouragement and assistance in bringing my story to the printed page.

TABLE OF CONTENTS

1   THE CATASTROPHE (AL NAKBA)   5

2   AROUND THE BRAZIER   10

3   A FAMILY DISPERSED   16

4   CAMP LIFE   23

5   A PEOPLE'S ARMY   37

6   NURSING THE ENEMY   47

7   ENCIRCLED   57

8   BACK TO BEIRUT   71

9   THE MASSACRE   81

10   NAWAL'S BROTHER   96

11   A TASTE OF FREEDOM   107

12   DOWN UNDER   117

13   BAR ELIAS   138

14   NEW LIFE   147

15   THE PROMISE OF OSLO   161

16   LIFE AND DEATH   171

17   WOMAN ON A MISSION   179

18   MY PERSONAL DIASPORA   184

EPILOGUE   RETURN TO TARSHIHA   191

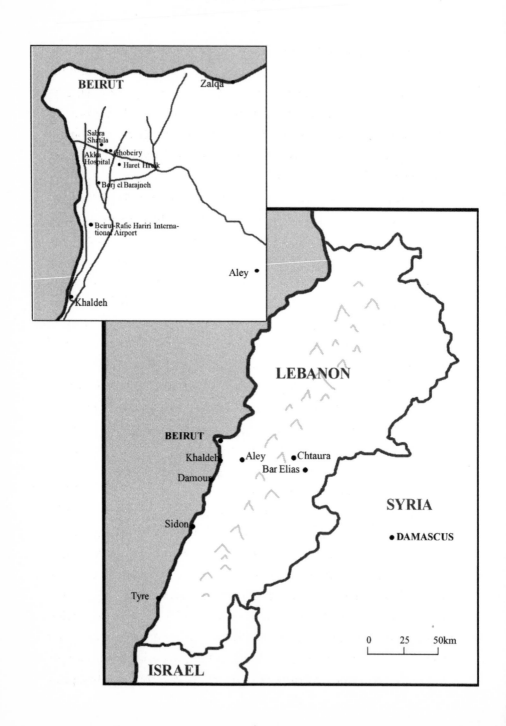

BEIRUT

Zalqa

Sabra
Shatila
Akka
Hospital
Ghobeiry
Haret Hreik
Borj el Barajneh

Beirut-Rafic Hariri International Airport

Aley

Khaldeh

LEBANON

BEIRUT

Khaldeh
Aley
Chtaura
Bar Elias
Damour

SYRIA

DAMASCUS

Sidon

Tyre

ISRAEL

0   25   50km

Introduction

Tears for Tarshiha is the story of my friend Dr Olfat Mahmoud who was born a refugee in Burj Barajneh, one of several Palestinian refugee camps in Beirut, Lebanon. I first met Olfat in 1982 having resigned my Middle Eastern consultancy with the World Health Organisation after the massacre of Palestinians in the Sabra and Shatila camps in Beirut. Olfat was a nurse in Gaza Hospital when I met her, and we soon became good friends.

Olfat's story is the story of hundreds of thousands of Palestinian refugees living in camps in Lebanon and throughout the Middle East, so it echoes the lives of millions of refugees worldwide. Through Olfat's story of leadership, extraordinary courage, dedication and resilience in war-torn Lebanon, we see the life of a refugee woman, nurse, mother, academic and outspoken advocate for her people who longs to return to her ancestral home and live in peace.

My friendship with Olfat has been sustained over the past 34 years initially though my work with Union Aid Aboard-APHEDA, then later through ongoing advocacy for refugees. It has been with Australian trade union support and Australian government funds that considerable development assistance has been provided not only to refugees in Lebanon but also to Palestinians living in the Occupied Territories.

Along with many others, for many years I had been urging Olfat to write her story. In March 2001 I spent six weeks with her, recorder in hand, reflecting on her life. Later, when she was in Australia, we did more interviews. In 2013 Dani Cooper conducted further interviews. It was an extremely emotional journey with lots of tears and laughter as Olfat recalled the trauma and joys of her life. I interviewed her mother, father, grandmothers and aunts as well as other family members living in the Burj Barajneh camp. I spoke, too, with Olfat's friends and colleagues. Using all the material, Dani Cooper has woven one woman's story of struggle for Palestinian rights, principal among them the right of return, into a personal narrative that captures Olfat's pain, exile, statelessness, and courage.

Seventy years on from the flight of Palestinians from their homeland, *Tears for Tarshiha* is a timely reminder of the present-day failure of the Middle East peace process and the failure of the international community through the United Nations to address the fate of some four million Palestinian refugees, to address the key issue of the Right of Return and to address the ongoing occupation of Palestinian territory.

Throughout her life Olfat has not ceased to fight for the principle, enshrined in international law and in numerous UN resolutions, of the Palestinian right of return. Her contribution to that principle has taken her all over the world, speaking about life in the camps and advocating for peace. In 2015 when she was invited to the UN in New York for a ceremony marking the formation of UNRWA. Speaking on behalf of Lebanese-based Palestinian refugees in the presence of the UN Secretary-General Ban Ki-moon, Olfat said:

> As a Palestine refugee in Lebanon, I have very limited rights, I am stateless, and I exist but am not recognised... My father and mother and my grandmothers and grandfathers and my children will remain refugees even if they marry Lebanese. For us the phrases 'human rights' and the 'right to be free from statelessness', and 'the right to live in dignity and safety' have lost all their meaning.

I hope this book will help raise understanding of the plight of Palestinian refugees and their rightful quest to return to their homeland.

Dr. Helen McCue AM,
Southern Highlands, NSW, Australia 2018.

1

THE CATASTROPHE (AL NAKBA)

I was not yet born, but on a winter's night on March 10, 1948, a group of 11 men I would never meet sealed my fate. On that Wednesday, these 11 men—Zionist leaders and young Jewish military officers—met near the seafront in northern Tel Aviv (*Tel al Rabia* in Arabic) at a rectangular, white building, ironically known as the 'Red House' in deference to its previous life as a workers' union headquarters. There they finalised the blueprint of a plan to systematically clear Palestinians from their homeland. Before the evening was over orders had been delivered to military units on the ground to prepare for the expulsion of Palestinians from large swathes of the region. It took six months to fulfil the mission and 'when it was over, more than half of Palestine's native population, close to 800,000 people, had been uprooted, 531 villages had been destroyed and 11 urban neighbourhoods emptied of their inhabitants'[1]. My village of Tarshiha, in northern Palestine, was among the last to be cleared. It was October 1948 and the military operation—what my people call *al Nakba*, the catastrophe—was by then concentrated on the Upper Galilee where my family had lived for centuries. As the Palestinian

---

1   Pappe, I. 2006, *The Ethnic Cleansing of Palestine*, One World Oxford, Preface.

men of our region fought back, the Israeli ground offensive was reinforced with an aerial bombardment.

❖ ❖ ❖

Today I can but imagine the terror my grandmother, *Alia*, felt as death rained from the sky, but the details of the day's events are etched in my memory—placed there through my grandparents' countless retellings to our family. In my mind I see my grandmother Alia racing back to the township from the fields, where she worked each day, with the roar of planes reverberating overhead. Milk from the jar she carries is splashing on to her clothing and face as she runs. Other women race beside her, stumbling at times as their feet catch in their long skirts, but propelled on by their terror and fears for their children. Smoke and dust rise from the village as the bombs fall. Alia hears the women's cries for their children as they run towards the devastation, her own voice echoing in the chorus.

As she arrives home, Alia races through the house calling for her children. There is no answer. Panic mounts. She runs next door and finds them huddled together, crying, with the neighbour and her family. Alia's oldest daughter, Hind, just 12, has her arms wrapped around her younger siblings. She falls into my grandmother's outstretched arms sobbing, 'Yamma, I've been praying for you to come back, I've been praying'.

Alia reluctantly pulls away from her children and runs towards the village centre where her sisters, cousins and other family members are sheltering in one of the few two-storey homes. 'Please Allah, keep them safe,' she pleads again and again out loud. 'Allah, let them be safe.' The village, which had survived since the days of the Phoenicians, is in ruins. Debris is everywhere: broken glass, rubble, and amidst the collapsed buildings, the wounded and dying. A young woman Alia recognises is lying on the ground, her legs blown off. A horse has been killed; human and animal flesh and blood mix together in death. Blood is splashed up the walls and soaking into the dusty road. And then she sees them—her niece and her beautiful four young boys. Dead. The shock barely registers before she races on. There is no time for grief, no time to mourn or bury the dead. There is time only for the living and to run.

Alia is now desperate to find her other relatives. Mahmoud, her husband, is on the eastern side of Tarshiha with his brothers and other men, trying to repel the Israeli ground troops. It is a vain hope—men with rifles and farm implements are no match for the well-armed Israeli troops. Every minute now counts as she seeks to stay one step ahead of the invaders. She is desperate to leave but won't go without her family. At last she finds them in one of the village's churches. Muslims and Christians—Palestinians all—crowded together, praying their place of sanctuary will not be hit. Alia's Christian neighbours beg her to stay, but she knows what can happen to those who linger when the Israelis march in. In Deir Yassin, just six months earlier, more than 100 men, women and children had been murdered by Israeli paramilitaries.[2] The massacre reverberated across Palestine and fuelled the flight of hundreds of Palestinians from their homes as the Israelis advanced. The same fear takes hold in Tarshiha.

Now reunited with her family, Alia gathers her children and collects a few items from home. She feeds the chickens, locks the house and puts the key, and a few pieces of jewellery and gold, inside the folds of her dress. With her children, sisters and other family, she heads to Tarshiha's western edge, to avoid the advancing Israeli army, and flees north towards Lebanon, 20 kilometres away.

She would never return. To this day I wonder if, as she walked away, my grandmother glanced back momentarily for one last glimpse of home. I hope so, but I doubt she realised she was walking into exile. Instead I expect Alia simply heaved her load more firmly on to her shoulders, shushed the children and head down, pushed forward to safety.

---

2   Israeli historian Benny Morris argued in *Birth of the Palestinian Problem Revisited* that news of the killings at Deir Yassin spread fear among Palestinians and encouraged many of them to flee their villages when attacked. It is a widely accepted view (http://bit.ly/NYTimes19980409).

❖❖❖

Of course, my family are not the only ones fleeing. There are hundreds of people on the move. Alia sees old people struggling to walk but cannot help as she carries her two youngest. As they flee, Israeli planes swoop low, harassing and terrifying them, pushing them to leave Palestine. Everyone is sure they will be bombed at any moment. When the planes approach, they run off the dusty road, pulling the children near to protect them. Often, they walk through olive groves and orchards, where branches scratch their bodies. Cousin Ahmed, who trades in Lebanon, arrives and guides villagers along the safest and quickest route. But still their constant companion remains the fear of being shot and killed.

On their first night of flight, my grandmother's family lies in the fields among olive trees, sheltering as best they can. Alia doles out the olives, cheese and bread she has grabbed from the house. There is momentary joy the next day when my grandfather Mahmoud rejoins the family, bringing with him some of the family's sheep and cows. But he also delivers the news that Tarshiha is lost.

The family continues its forced trek towards Lebanon, finally reaching its borders on the third day. Alia now realises the extent of the exodus with thousands of Palestinians crossing the border. For three days more they continue to walk, and by now the flight is taking its toll. While the days are warm, the nights in the open fields are cold. Alia's youngest son, Ahmad, not yet weaned, dies from pneumonia. Muhammad, just shy of two, soon follows. In the Islamic faith the dead are buried as soon as possible, so the two baby boys are laid to rest in an unmarked grave in the fields, time only for a short ceremony and prayers. Weighed down with grief, Alia continues on her forced march to the village of Aita Al Sha'b. There, she is reunited with other families who join the trek on to Qana and Burj el Shamalie, where they finally rest.

It has been six days and it is only now Alia and her family learn that the Israeli army has occupied Palestine. Still, Alia remains confident they will soon return home. She has her house key and their animals. Fields will soon need tending. What would the Israelis want with her home? But this certainty is shattered when Alia's grandfather, worrying over what has been left behind, decides to return to Tarshiha. The fighting is over, and he is an old, unarmed man. But that is of no consequence. The order in Israel is to shoot anyone who tries to return, and he is killed in his attempt to cross the border. Alia understands at last that the road home is closed.

Our exile has begun.

2

AROUND THE BRAZIER

Although I was born there, I have always known Lebanon is not my home. I am Palestinian and although I have never been home I know my land intimately—its smells, its landscapes, its tastes, its history. It is embedded in the deepest reaches of my psyche, imprinted in my DNA. Every winter's night in Burj Barajneh, the refugee camp in the southern suburbs of Beirut where I was born, I would make the journey back to Palestine as I sat with my family trying to keep warm by the brazier. With the glowing embers shadowing their faces, my grandparents—Alia and Mahmoud—would tell me, my brothers, sisters and cousins, of their life in Tarshiha. Even as the Israeli government on the international stage denied the very existence of Palestine, my grandparents would breathe it back to life around the fires. And each night they would promise us that we would one day return to our homeland.

Tarshiha—the name is like a breath on the wind, but in fact it invokes a famous Arabic warrior, who died fighting the Crusaders. Our village, like many in the Galilee, reached back into history. Its narrow stone-cobbled streets held tales of biblical times, the arrival of the Crusaders in the 12th century and the rule of the Ottoman Empire in the 1500s. The surrounding mountains and rocky fields had been toiled for generations, home to ancient olive groves up to 4000 years old and rows of citrus trees.

When my grandmother told us stories of the village, I had an inkling of habits and customs unchanged with the passing of time. She wove a picture in words of young women working together on their family's land growing fruit and vegetables, gossiping and laughing as they toiled. My mother, Hind, she would reveal, helped as a young girl to build beehives, and the white honey from the bees was a delicacy shared with family, friends and neighbours in the *dar* (an open-air square in the front or centre of the house).

My grandparents, like most families, kept animals for meat and milk and with the crops they grew were relatively self-sufficient—everything was homegrown and homemade. They would barter with their neighbours or use their produce to pay for needed services.

Like many villagers, however, the family's main source of income was tobacco—a crop introduced by the British in the 1920s. Traders would visit the farm to buy the tobacco, but Alia's father also sold tobacco in Haifa, strapping the crop on to donkeys and walking the beast to the port city 50 kilometres away. After a successful sale, as was the custom, he would slaughter a sheep and distribute the meat to the poor in the village.

◈◈◈

While my grandmother wove her tale of food and family, my grandfather was determined we know our history and the battles our people had fought to remain on their land. He was better than any encyclopaedia and, long before a television entered the refugee camp, he was our main source of entertainment. Leaning in towards us, the firelight shadowing his face, my grandfather evoked our country's past, taking us back to the days when our village was ruled from Constantinople, to our more recent history as a bargaining chip in international diplomacy. He would outline the circumstances in which Palestine had been 'gifted' in the aftermath of World War I to the British as a protectorate under the Sykes-Picot Agreement[3], his tone mocking the international leaders who believed we were a present to be wrapped and handed on.

Then he would push himself back and sit tall, chest swollen with pride, meeting each of our eyes as he described the Palestinian resistance to the British occupation and Jewish migration in the early 1920s and 1930s. 'We were determined not to live under the yoke of the British and we fought hard for our independence and freedom,' he would declare, the unspoken message that we had to fight again. I remember my excitement on hearing how our village of Tarshiha was actively involved in this resistance, including the 1936 national uprising as well as the general revolt that lasted until 1939. But my grandfather would point out that the price of this resistance was high. Many people from Tarshiha were among the dead or imprisoned.

These nights by the small coal fire were replicated around the refugee camp as our history was orally passed on to a new generation. Other relatives would visit our gathering and add their memories to these history lessons. My grandmother's sister-in-law, Umm Samir, had lived through the British raids on the village and would bring the memory to life as she re-enacted the warning call, 'It is cloudy, it is cloudy'. This alluded to the dust storms created by the soldiers on horseback, letting everyone know the British were coming. The soldiers would order the women into the mosque and the men to a large garage. They would search their homes and interrogate them. During these raids, the British took the women's scarves and put them on their heads, making fun of their dress. And we all laughed when Umm Samir told us the only two words in English she could remember were, 'come out, come out' as the British soldiers rounded them up.

On these nights Mahmoud would always remind us that Palestine was a multi-faith society of Muslims, Christians and Jews. In

---

[3] The Sykes-Picot Agreement between Britain and France of 1916 envisioned Palestine, at the collapse of the Ottoman Empire, as part of an International Zone. Arthur Balfour, the British Foreign Secretary, issued the Balfour Declaration in 1917 that promised to establish 'a Jewish national homeland in Palestine'. The British mandate lasting from 1920 to 1948 was formally endorsed by the League of Nations in 1922.

Tarshiha the Friday call to prayers at the mosque gave way to the peel of church bells on Sunday. Palestinian Jewish Arabs had been part of our society since ancient times and shared our language and culture. Their family doctor was a Palestinian Jew, while the Christians worked mostly as goldsmiths, carpenters and blacksmiths or merchants. We had lived in peace with each other for centuries, he would say, quietly adding as if in a plea, that our war was against the colonisers, not each other.

In Mahmoud's version of history the ultimate act of betrayal was actually quite recent. He would point to 1937 and the British Peel Commission that recommended the partition of Palestine. With a vote by a Parliament in London our village, Tarshiha, was arbitrarily determined by the British occupiers to go to the Jewish migrants[4]. When he spoke these words Mahmoud's voice would shake with anger. 'Of course, we resisted this outrageous idea and we fought the British again; but thousands of us were killed or arrested'.

His anger with the British was soon directed at another 'enemy'—the United Nations. In the aftermath of World War II, the newly formed UN decided that Palestine should be divided in two, giving the Arabs and Jews each a state[5]. 'Our rights as the owners of Palestinian land were not considered,' he would say, his voice loud with anger as he held his large hands against his chest as if to quell the pain. The Zionist Jews liked this decision even less than our people and responded with violence: assassinating the UN's Swedish peace negotiator and attacking Palestinian organisations, banks, railways and industrial installations. Many Palestinian civilians lost their lives.

'We fought again, against the British and the Jewish settlers, but we were poorly armed and poorly organised as many of our best

4   The British Peel Commission or the Palestine Royal Commission was established in 1936 after the 1936-39 revolt, and in its 1937 report, recommended partition of Palestine.
5   The UN resolution 181 (11) of 29 November 1947, recommended that an independent Arab State alongside a Jewish State be established, and that there be a Special International Regime for the city of Jerusalem.

leaders had been killed or imprisoned by the British,' my grandfather would add with great despondency.

It would be nice to say our fireside stories had a happy ending—but no matter which new detail my grandfather added, we all knew what the last page of his 'history' would reveal. On May 14, 1948, Jewish forces declared the state of Israel and their campaign to eradicate our presence from our homeland began.

At times my grandparents would set politics aside and our fireside conversations would give us an insight into Palestinian customs and their early married life. My grandparents were cousins and grew up together, often meeting at family celebrations. It was quite common at the time for cousins to wed, so with their parents' permission they were married in the early 1930s. Their first home in Tarshiha was a large house with many rooms, bought from a Palestinian journalist who had left the country after being persecuted by the British. The house was two storeys and too big for my grandmother's family alone, so she rented out one floor. Tarshiha was one of the larger villages in the district and was proud of the fact it had two schools, including a secondary school. Palestinians strongly believed that education was important for girls, so when Alia's daughters, my mother Hind among them, were old enough, they went to school as did all the other girls in the village. However, because of the war my mother was never able to complete her education—a sadness both she and my grandmother carried through their lives.

My grandmother often talked about relatives and people she had known in Palestine, including Umm Salim. When she died in 1947, the year before their flight, the whole community, Christian and Muslim, supported one another. People in Tarshiha came and sat with the family, visitors being offered bitter coffee as was the custom. The women of the family bathed Umm Salim and buried her within 24 hours which is required for Muslims. Some of the village women performed a special dance on the first three days of mourning—called *nadib*—in which they carried scarves in their hands and waved them about, shouting, crying out and speaking to Umm

Salim: remembering her wonderful sense of humour, her work in the village, her role as a mother and wife, and her friendship. They would alternate this ritual with religious songs.

Relatives and friends brought food to the family, and those who could afford it slaughtered sheep and distributed the meat among the villagers. On the third day of this mourning period, they distributed a small pastry filled with crushed mixed nuts or dates, known as *ma'moul*. This practice was repeated on the 40th day after the funeral, when the sweets were offered with bitter coffee. During the period of mourning, all foods eaten at times of celebration such as *kibbeh*, were forbidden, as was celebratory music.

Stories of our homeland were often accompanied by the food of our land. On these cold nights by the fire, my mother would make us a special Palestinian sweet where she would mix flour, water and sugar, and bring it to the boil while stirring all the time. Then, when this mixture had thickened she would pour it onto a tray and make a hole in the middle into which she would place a piece of butter and some sugar. The sugar and butter would melt, and we would eat the dripping hot 'custard' with great relish. This sweet dish, called *a'ccedi*, is famous in our culture and also has special religious significance: Omar, one of the Prophet Muhammad's key followers, is said to have made this dish for a poor family. As children we loved these sweets and, even though my parents were not overly religious, we were comforted by the place this dish played in our religious history. To this day, it remains one of my favourite foods.

3

A FAMILY DISPERSED

In their flight from Tarshiha in 1948, members of my extended family scattered to either Lebanon or Syria. My grandparents planned to join Alia's brothers and uncles in Aleppo, Syria, but by then the Syrian government had taken its quota of refugees and closed its border. So the family was split, with my grandparents marooned in Lebanon. It was just the first of many separations to come.

The family's first 'home' in Lebanon was a canvas tent that, when erected, was the size of a small room. For the four freezing, wet winter months of 1948-49 a dozen of my grandparents' family lived in this basic dwelling in northern Lebanon. The only bedding they'd brought from home was one small mattress and a pillow for the babies. But with their sheep, cows, cash and gold jewellery, they were more fortunate than many others. Some refugees with money in the banks in Palestine could not withdraw it. Many had left in panic with just the clothes they were wearing. When word began to spread through the camps that Jewish settlers were moving into their homes, my grandparents and their peers were devastated by the news. They had not just lost their homeland, they had lost their home, their belongings, everything.

By February 1949, my grandparents had moved south to Burj Barajneh, a UN-run refugee camp in bushland on the edge of cosmopolitan Beirut. Here they at last found themselves among friends, people from Tarshiha and nearby villages. The camps quickly established themselves into little villages, so even in exile we lived alongside our old neighbours. These tent cities spread as far as the eye could see, with little in the way of amenities or distractions for those it housed.

I can't imagine how confronting this new life was for my mother, who at that time was just entering her teenage years. The security and tranquility of her village life was gone; in its stead she faced a life of uncertainty and deprivation.

My mother has spoken about the long, winter nights when the wind blew furiously around the camp tents. She would wake and, with her brothers and sisters, struggle desperately to stop their meagre shelter from being blown into the sea. The small earth channel around the tent inevitably failed to keep the water out and they often had to work furiously to keep their bedding, mattresses and precious few clothes dry. Amid all the shouting as people held the tent down, the children would be crying with cold and despair. The sleet and icy winds from the snow-clad mountains to the east of Beirut drove the chill deep into their bones. My mother believed her later severe arthritis was a legacy of those early days in the tent.

'It was so cold in the winter. I was never warm enough sleeping on a mattress on that hard, cold, damp floor. And the heat and humidity of the summer was equally unbearable,' she would recall.

While their hearts were always yearning for home, my grandparents were determined to keep on with life. At first the floor of their tent was only sand, but after a short while my grandparents made a hard mud floor. They cooked over a small fire, a *babboor*, fuelled with petrol, but for years many people cooked on open fires outside, using wood gathered from the bush nearby. Soon after they arrived, my grandfather also built a mudbrick bakery in which the family and neighbours would bake food in the traditional Palestinian village way.

Subsistence was an everyday chore for those in the camp. Collecting water was a tedious daily task for the young ones, including my mother. The public toilet and washing facilities were a seven-minute walk from the family tent and everyone had to make this trek on freezing winter nights, and in the summer heat and humidity when the sand would burn their feet. For seven years they lived like this— and always at the front of their mind was the conviction that any day, they would return home. It was not an unrealistic belief and one in which the international community was complicit: just two months after my family left Tarshiha, on December 11, 1948, the United Nations General Assembly passed Resolution 194:

> The UN General Assembly resolves that the refugees wishing to return to their homes and live at peace with their neigh- bours should be permitted to do so at the earliest practicable date, and that compensation should be paid for the property of those choosing not to return and for the loss of, or damage to property which under the principles of international law and in equity should be made good by the government or author- ities responsible.[6]

When my family and all the hundreds of thousands of Palestinian refugees heard this news, they were joyous as they understood it meant they would soon be going home. But even as the UN voted, Israel was working against the order. In Palestine all traces of our people's existence were being erased. Parks were built on former Palestinian land, cemeteries became playgrounds[7] and Palestinian homes were occupied by Zionist settlers. On December 8, 1949, just short of a year after its bold declaration that Palestinians had the right of return, the UN Relief and Works Agency for Palestinian Refugees in the Near East (UNRWA) was founded—a clear indi- cation the international community had little interest in enforcing Resolution 194.

---

6 United Nations General Assembly 194 (III). *Palestine: Progress Report of the United Nations Mediator*, A/RES/194 (III)11 December 1948.
7 Pappe, I. 2006, *Ethnic Cleansing*, p. 142, Plates 16-17.

Until its establishment, Palestinian refugees were supported by the International Committee of the Red Cross and similar bodies.[8] UNRWA's mandate was to provide for the almost one million Palestinian refugees who had fled Israel. Many felt, however, that by building hospitals, schools and improving conditions in the camp, UNRWA was actually further entrenching our exile.

◈◈◈

My family's flight from Palestine had a major impact on my mother's education. She became one of the many thousands of children who, due to the war and their exile, missed years of schooling. In spite of her parents' commitment to her education, my mother never went back to school, instead, working to help the family survive. My grandfather, like many men in the camp, worked as a farm labourer for a Christian who owned land not far from the camp. He earned a small income and was able to grow food, but there was little money left for other essential things. When I was little I remember each day around 4 o'clock, my siblings and I would race to the camp's edge to meet him on his return from work as he always had a 'gift' of corn or other food for his grandchildren.

When my mother was just 13 a fellow refugee offered to teach her how to use a pedal sewing machine. After learning this skill, my teenage mother rented a machine for her own use and in the cramped confines of the family tent began to make embroidered sheets and pillowcases. Once completed, she would walk for more than an hour to the shops in Beirut to sell this beautiful and much-sought-after handiwork.

There was little social life in the camp except for the numerous weddings to which all our extended family and friends from villages

---

8   In November 1948, the UN established the United Nations Relief for Palestine Refugees (UNRPR) to support Palestine refugees and coordinate efforts of NGOs and other UN bodies. On Dec 8, 1949, the UN General Assembly established the United Nations Relief and Works Agency for Palestine Refugees in the Near East (UNRWA) under Resolution 302 (IV). The agency inherited the assets of the UNRPR and took over the Red Cross refugee registration records.

around Tarshiha were invited. It was at one such wedding that my mother met her future husband, Khalil. As both their families were from Tarshiha, Hind and Khalil had met several times before but barely knew each other. However, at the wedding an interest was sparked. I am not surprised by the instant attraction. My mother was stunningly beautiful despite the hardship under which she was raised. Her thick, shoulder-length black hair framed a striking, dignified face with dark, warm eyes. Likewise, my father was the personification of tall, dark and handsome. Dressed in their western clothes, they could have been any cosmopolitan couple strolling the boulevards of Paris or Londson. As our customs decree, Khalil's parents asked my grandparents if their son could marry Hind. My grandparents were happy to support their courtship. Khalil worked as an accountant with a firm that sold cars in the mostly Christian sector of East Beirut, earning 95 lira a week, which was considered a good wage, and certainly enough to support a wife and family. But most importantly my grandparents could see Hind and Khalil cared for one another. With her parents' approval, in 1955, after spending six years, or a third of her life, living in a tent, my mother, aged 19, married and finally moved into a home.

It was a momentous occasion for them and the family as they were among the first in Burj camp to move out of their tented homes into a constructed shelter. It was very basic but by camp standards they were comfortably off. My mother had a family right away; my eldest brother, Nader, was born in 1956; Ihab came two years later and I followed in 1960. We were all delivered in the house with a minimum of fuss—attended by women from the camp with a local *daya* or midwife to help during the birth. Becoming a parent did not slow my mother down. She was fiercely independent and determined to contribute, so even though she had babies on the hip and in the womb, she continued to sell her Palestinian embroidery, setting up her own small business with girls from the camp to do the sewing.

The 'house' where I was born consisted of one small room and was made of mud walls with a corrugated iron roof. A tiny kitchen was attached, and in the tradition of our houses in Palestine, there was an outside area that we called the *dar,* a walled, open-air court-yard. With a government ban on refugees bringing materials into the camp our homes were made from mud, concrete blocks and scraps of iron that we could find nearby. As a result nothing fitted neatly together. Despite our best efforts the wind and rain would seek out the gaps and make their way into our home as a constant companion. During the day our mattresses would be piled in the corner and at night spread out for sleeping. But sleep was often hard to come by. On rainy, winter nights the cold would go to my bones and as new leaks would emerge in the roof, my parents would wake us to move the mattresses so we would not get wet.

Summer brought no relief as the stifling heat also made sleep near impossible, and the wild cats fighting on the tin roof at night made certain any shut-eye was temporary. Our house had no electricity. My mother cooked over a gas stove. All the washing was, of course, done by hand. There was no bathroom and no shower. We used to have our bath in the kitchen, which, with only a curtain as the door, opened out into the *dar.* My mother would boil water on a gasoline stove and the children would be washed in a wide bowl. The minute we were told we had to bath, we would cry, especially in winter. What should have been a pleasurable experience was for us a misery to be dispensed with as quickly as possible.

During this time all camp residents had to use public toilets as private toilets were banned. This ban was symbolic of the Lebanese Government's attitude toward the Palestinian refugees reinforcing the view that we were not welcome. From our arrival in 1948 we were denied basic services, and access to employment was severely restricted. Unlike those who fled to Jordan where many were given citizenship, and to Syria where they were given civil rights such as access to education, health care and jobs, Palestinians in Lebanon were, and remain, stateless second-class citizens. But as in all bad situations, there are ways and there are ways. My father had good relations with the owner of the company where he worked, and with his help, he was able to get special permission from the government for a private toilet for our small house. It was no luxurious affair, just a small hole in the ground in a tiny space off the main room. This hole led to a common pit outside which had to be emptied manually because there was no sewer system. It was a great improvement for the family and meant we no longer had to walk for seven minutes through the camp to the public toilet.

Our joy over this 'improvement' was profound, but again highlighted how our expectations were being held hostage. At a time when the first McDonald's was being built in the US and motor cars and trams jostled for position on the city streets of Beirut, we lived as if in another age. Just a few blocks away the conveniences of modern life were plentiful in Beirut, then known as the Paris of the Middle East. But not for us the coffee in the cafes and strolls along the beachside boulevard, instead we had to play the grateful visitor. I can remember when I was little, UNRWA representatives would bring visitors to our house when they wanted to show them how clean the camp was. We were model refugees, well-behaved and spotless but we were stateless, with no passport, no country to go to and no future.

4

CAMP LIFE

My early childhood was punctuated by critical regional events that impacted greatly on my life as a Palestinian in Lebanon. In the early 1950s, Gamal Abdel Nasser, a popular resistance leader in Egypt and strong supporter of the Palestinian cause, led the fight against the British occupation of Egypt that resulted in Egyptian independence in 1954. Tensions in the Middle East were exacerbated in 1956 when Nasser, now Egyptian President, nationalised the Suez Canal, threatening petroleum shipments from the Persian Gulf to western Europe and sparking an international crisis.[9] His ultimate victory in this action led to a growing pan-Arabic movement and in 1958, Egypt and Syria formed the short-lived United Arab Republic (UAR), a move supported by Muslims, including the Palestinians

---

9   The Suez crisis was provoked by a US and British decision not to help fund as promised the Aswan High Dam, in response to what they saw as growing ties between Egypt and the Soviet Union. When diplomatic efforts to settle the crisis failed, Britain and France secretly prepared military action to regain control of the canal, finding a ready ally in Israel whose troops invaded Egypt in November, advancing toward the canal. Britain and France, following their plan, demanded Israeli and Egyptian troops withdraw from the canal, and sent in troops to enforce a ceasefire ordered by the United Nations. Opposition to the action in the US and Europe led to a UN evacuation of British and French troops in December and Israeli forces withdrew in March 1957. Nasser emerged from the crisis a victor and a hero for the cause of Arab nationalism—*Encyclopedia Brittanica Online*.

in Lebanon. The success of this movement helped politicise our people and in response, a Palestinian leadership-in-exile emerged, supported by Syria and Egypt.

By contrast, the Lebanese Christian President Camille Chamoun was strengthening the country's ties with the British, French, US and Israel. Conflict over these regional events, the role of former colonisers, as well as fighting between Lebanon's influential political families—based largely along religious lines—contributed to the civil war that started in May 1958. Unable to contain the warring factions, Chamoun called in the US Marines. It was the first, but not the last time, the US Marines were in Lebanon.

There was no organised Palestinian resistance at this time and Palestinians in general stood apart from Lebanese politics during the 1950s and early 1960s. Nonetheless, the Lebanese police and internal security—the *Maktab Thani,* or Duexieme Bureau—kept a close eye on us. As a child, I was scared of the Lebanese police and security officers. They had an office at the entrance to the camp and were always in the camp strutting around. Just walking past them would set my heart racing; I was always afraid they would stop and question me. My family, like all Palestinians in Lebanon, was heavily constrained and we knew to keep our opinions on matters in Lebanon to ourselves.

The Maktab controlled the minutiae of our lives and seemed to revel in making life difficult and humiliating us. We needed permission for everything. If we wanted to visit relatives in another camp, or to travel in Lebanon, we needed to get a special pass. If we wanted to hold a celebration, we needed special permission. I vividly remember my father hammering a nail into the wall of our house as he tried to hang a picture. Suddenly, the police were there, demanding to know what he was doing—despite it being self-evident. My father calmly replied he was just hanging a picture. They asked to see his permission note for the 'improvement to the house'. He was then taken away. And although the police held him away for just half an hour, for all of us it was 30 minutes of real fear that he would never return.

One of the cruellest restrictions imposed on us in these times, however, related to the use of water. When my parents lived in tents, UNRWA used to bring water in tanks for the camp residents. After people became more settled, UNRWA connected the camp to the main city water lines but installed only a few communal watering points in the camp. People then had to fetch water by hand from these points. When I was a child there was no proper system of wastewater disposal. We had to throw all wastewater into the drains that ran through the narrow lanes of the camp. The Maktab banned any water to be thrown in the streets during the day so we had to collect wastewater in large bowls and to wait until nighttime to dispose of it. By then, of course, the bowls were full and heavy. This meant the women in the camp had to wash their children, their clothes and clean their houses after dark. As we did not have electricity, all of this had to be done by gasoline light.

This meant I had an uneasy relationship with water as a child. My mother scolded me if I played with water and would say, with total justification, 'They [the police] will put me or your father in jail and they will beat us'. This terrified me. One day my mother went to visit a sick neighbour. My older brothers were playing with some water in a bowl in the *dar* and did not realise the water was splashing and draining away into the lane outside the house. There was a bang on the door and then the Maktab officers were calling for my mother, who came running from the neighbour's.

'Don't you know that it is forbidden to have water spilling into the camp in the daytime!' the officer yelled.

'I am sorry. I wasn't at home,' she replied. 'I was visiting my neighbour who is sick. And, look, they're only little children.'

My mother was lucky that day, as she was only threatened, but it added to the feeling of insecurity and intimidation she always felt. Often women were taken to the police station for spilling water during the early hours of the morning, when it was light, because they could not finish their housework during the night. They were not arrested, but at the station police officers would beat them on the feet and threaten them with worse. So, my mother was right to be afraid.

◇◇◇

Burj Barajneh camp was built on a hill in an undeveloped, sparsely inhabited, agricultural area south of Beirut. Long before the airport was built nearby, the area was a vacant wasteland dotted with pine groves that have long since disappeared. On one side of the camp there was a sand hill where children would go and play, but it was crowded so my siblings and I rarely went there. Instead, I used to play at home with my brothers, Ihab and Nader, and my sister Mervat, who was two years younger than me. My mother made us dolls and we would play make-believe games such as doctors and nurses, like children anywhere in the world.

Compared with many children in the camp at that time, we were relatively well off. Some people could not afford food and relied on neighbours to feed them. My father had a good job throughout most of my childhood and occasionally bought us toys in addition to those my mother made. But we were also very creative in the way we invented games and we made our own toys from bits of wood and things that we could find around the camp. Because we had little space in the house or the *dar*, we had to make our games fit into this small area. Playing hide and seek was not much fun as we had few places to hide. Instead we would play other games with our fingers and toes, sitting around in a small circle. One game my aunts taught us involved sitting in a circle with our feet pointing to the middle. We would pass a small parcel around and sing:

> *My grandmother sent me to get a pomegranate.*
> *I brought it, it fell down and broke.*
> *Oh, oh, oh, bride, hide your foot in the box.*

In Palestine, when girls get married, they prepare a big wooden chest with clothes and other things needed for the marriage, a bridal 'chest'. This song was about that tradition. When we stopped singing, the person who ended up with the parcel would be number one in the circle and from there we would count to 10. The person who got the number 10 had to tuck one leg under their body or hide it under their clothes. When both legs were hidden you were out of the game.

I spent most of the time with my brothers and sisters playing these types of games. We never fought, although naturally we had different personalities. Nader was very quiet and obedient, but Ihab was stubborn and somewhat wilful. As a young girl, I was quiet but strong and used to follow my mother, carrying the mop and broom, wanting to help her. Because I was my father's oldest daughter, I held a special place in his heart and was a little spoiled by him. He gave me the rare Arabic name, Olfat, which means to care and love or cherish.

So, my childhood memories are filled with this sense of security within my family, but they are also filled with memories of the daily insecurity of our lives in the camp. My family's talk was often filled with grief and longing. Trapped in the misery and deprivation of the camp, they longed for the sight and smell of their fields: the olive groves, the trees and the fresh air of their home in Tarshiha. And that longing was passed on to me.

As much as the older people in the camp wanted to return home, life went on and there were many joyous times. When I was around six years, my aunt Amne was married. Weddings were a time of great celebration in the camp and I can still remember her party in great detail. Two chairs, one for the bride and one for the groom, were placed on a large table behind which there was a beautiful carpet, for decoration. There was a lot of drumming and traditional singing and Amne, dressed in a gorgeous red gown, sat while the women sang, and men and women danced the traditional *Dabkeh*.

After some time, my mother and her other sisters helped Amne down from the table and took her away. She soon reappeared dressed in a beautiful blue dress. This happened seven times, each time Amne came dressed in a gown of vibrant colours, until at the last she appeared in a white bridal gown. The tradition of changing dresses enabled the bride to take to the marriage seven gowns that she would use for other public celebrations and other people's weddings. As a new bride, Amne was expected to dress well, and her husband would have paid for these dresses as part of the marriage dowry. The more the bride changed her clothes, the more people would talk all summer, 'Oh yes, she changed dresses five or eight times'. Or they might say, 'What a generous husband she has as he had to pay for all these dresses'.

Before this public marriage party, the couple had exchanged a marriage contract in the presence of a Muslim Sheik and two witnesses. This religious ceremony constituted the official marriage. This official marriage was followed by the marriage party, which signified the time from when the couple lived together as husband and wife. At this public wedding party, when Amne came at last dressed in her exquisite white wedding gown, her groom joined her. He took her wedding ring, which she had worn on her right hand following the formal religious marriage several months earlier, and placed it on her left hand, and she repeated the same ritual with him, placing his ring on his left hand. This movement of the wedding rings to each other's left hands meant that they were officially married, and the public wedding party continued with much dancing and singing for many hours, with everyone joining in, children included.

The special wedding food all the women had prepared was brought out after the service and my eyes boggled at the feast before me. Large trays of rice and meat, and rice and chicken, both covered with nuts were laid out. Later *mlebbes,* sugared almonds, were offered as people danced and enjoyed the celebration. For the wedding, we wore our best clothes which we had received at the end of Ramadan, a key Islamic feast. It was such a treat for us to have new clothes, that we would sleep with them beside us, and put our new shoes under our pillows so they wouldn't run away. My mother made all our clothes and was expert at re-purposing things. If something was worn or too small, she would cut it and remake it as curtains or cushion covers. Everything was recycled.

Until I was six, my life was contained within the camp boundaries, and I was only dimly aware of the city that lay at our doorstep. All that changed when I started school as the UNRWA-run
schools for Palestinians were outside the camp. It was then that I saw
shops and cars and 'normal' houses; and began to ask why we didn't
live in these nice places. My mother would patiently remind me that
Lebanon was not our country. I wondered how we could live in Lebanon but not be from that country; after all I was born there. I would
ask, 'Why am I here if this is not my country?' My mother would say,
'Because we had to leave our country; we were forced to leave Palestine'. Even when this was explained, I found it hard to understand.

Happily for me, my mother refused to let me do housework because she wanted her children to focus on their education—a legacy
I think of her missing out on schooling. Our neighbours criticised
her, but she would say to them, 'Olfat will learn these things when
she marries'. But I also sensed it was her contribution to the fight for
Palestine as she truly believed through education we would regain
our country.

Every day when we arrived home from school just after 2 o'clock,
my mother would have lunch ready. Then, and after everything was
cleared away, we would all sit together on the floor around a small
round table and, holding my baby brother Amer, she would check
our homework, correct it and quiz us on what we had learnt. Early
the next morning she would go over this material again and then we
had to repeat our homework with her. I often believe the foundation
for my later academic success was laid in those days, and I copied her
approach when I had my own children.

Thanks to my father's job, we were one of the first families in the
camp to get a gas cooker and we were the first also to get a radio.
People would come and congratulate us on these new purchases, and
were happy for us, but we always made sure we shared these luxu-
ries. My mother told me that in the late 1950s, whenever Egyptian
President Nasser was giving a speech on radio our house became a
gathering place and would be crowded with camp residents who

came to listen. Our people lauded Nasser as a hero for defeating the British and for his support of our struggle: we were convinced that he would help us to return home. It was via this radio that the world came into our camp and, as long as it was not too loud, the Lebanese police kept an eye on us from a distance and did not confiscate it.

Huddled around this technology, the family could hear first-hand of the global events impacting on our lives. Internationally, the Cold War between the US and the USSR was in full swing, each super-power vying for influence in the Middle East. By 1964, the Arab League had belatedly started to support the Palestinians with the establishment of the Palestinian Liberation Organisation (PLO). For the first time we had a formal, regional political voice; and in the camps, students', women's and other representative groups were formed, and began to agitate politically. Yasser Arafat, living with his Palestinian parents in Cairo, established a more radical group, *Al-Fatah*, ('The Opening') which was outside the Arab-sponsored PLO. Arafat's group was committed to armed struggle for the liberation of Palestine, but in time he took over the PLO and became its chairman.

As these groups began to bring our situation to international attention, our hopes of returning home were once more cruelly shattered. The 1967 war between Israel and the Arab nations led to the decimation and humiliation of the Arab armies. Israel now occupied the Palestinian territories of the Gaza Strip and the West Bank, including all of Jerusalem, as well as the Syrian Golan Heights and the Egyptian Sinai Peninsula. Thousands of lives were lost, and another 100,000 Palestinians were displaced, with most crossing from the West Bank into Jordan. Many were forcibly evicted from their homes and their villages bulldozed to prevent their return. In November 1967, UN Security Council Resolution 242 reaffirmed the right of return of all Palestinians to their homeland. But once again Israel ignored the decree and the world assented through its silence.

In Lebanon these regional events split the country. Arabs, the progressive Orthodox Christians and the Communist Party supported

Nasser's pan-Arabism and the Palestinians. On the other side were the pro-western Christians of East Beirut. Nationally, there was also serious conflict amongst Lebanese over the growing economic disparity between country and city. The decades-long political and religious tensions inside Lebanon needed little fuelling while inside Burj Barajneh camp, Palestinian resistance, and support for that resistance, were growing.

I was in my second year of school that year and on a chore to buy tomato paste made in the camp by local women. I was in the tiny lane outside our house when two men in the black and white *keffiyyeh*, the traditional Arab scarf worn by males, approached. I could only see their eyes and I screamed in terror. My mother rushed outside. The poor men wanted to calm me but my mother, aware of the danger they were in, told them to run. She turned to me and bent down looking directly into my eyes, whispering urgently, 'You are allowed to lie now. Tell anyone who comes that you saw a dog and were afraid.'

I did not understand. My mother had always told me not to lie. In what seemed just seconds later, two Lebanese Army officers came running down the lane towards us. I was in tears. They asked me why I was crying.

'I was frightened by a dog,' I hastily replied.

That seemed to satisfy them because they moved away, but I was worried by the incident and later asked my mother why she had told me to lie. She sought to ease my concerns and said, 'It is forbidden to lie, but in this situation what you said was a white lie. Those soldiers were chasing those two young men you saw because they are fighting to liberate Palestine.' She added, 'If the Lebanese capture them they will torture them and put them in prison, so we want to protect them, not harm them'.

She told me to tell no one outside our family. Young though I was, I realised what she was asking me to do was important, and I obeyed.

My parents were not political within the PLO but they supported anyone who could help them return home. I asked my parents many questions about these young men and why they had covered their faces. My father explained they needed to remain anonymous because they were soldiers fighting to take us back to our homeland in Palestine.

'The Lebanese government does not want them here,' he said.

When I asked why they would support a war and killing, it was my mother who answered.

'Look at how we are living here in this refugee camp—in one miserable small room. Back in Palestine we have a large house and huge lands; our house and land are still there. Lebanon is not our home. All we want is to go back to the decent life we had before. These young men are here to protect us from the Lebanese government that is making our lives even more miserable. We're doing nothing here. We're just existing in this terrible place.'

That was a turning point in my life as it opened my eyes to our armed struggle. It was from those years that I began to realise we had to fight to liberate Palestine. I saw that my mother was right. Why should she do all the housework at night and early in the morning just because the Lebanese police said so? Why did we have no space to play in? Why should we tolerate being treated without respect; and why should we allow our people to be harassed, intimidated, tortured and killed? My family and all the camp residents supported these young fighters, the *feda'yeen,* in any way we could. We would give them olives, *halaweh,* and tins of whatever we had. My mother and all the women would knit socks, jumpers, hats and scarves in military green wool and send them to the fighters. All the refugees wanted to do everything they could to help the struggle to return to Palestine.

Around this time an incident occurred that brought home to me just how vulnerable we were. Uncle Ahmad, my mother's brother, was a journalist on a local paper in Beirut. One night he failed to come home. My relatives searched for him and eventually found him in prison, arrested because an article he wrote about the PLO upset the Lebanese security forces. The Lebanese owner of the newspaper that published his article was not accused of any crime, but my uncle was in prison for more than a year. I was very close to him and during his incarceration, the family feared for his safety. My grandmother used to visit him every day and we worked hard with local lawyers to have him freed. After his release, my uncle was expelled from Lebanon, and I remember wondering why we should suffer like this. My uncle's was not an isolated case, of course. We all knew the price of speaking out in Lebanon about our struggle for freedom.

Lebanon in the late 1960s was ripe for revolution. Lebanese unions, students and leftist organisations became more vocal and active in their fight against social inequalities. The two key issues were economic disparity and political dominance by the Christians, the latter being a legacy of the first National Pact, set up by the French colonial power that created Lebanon's 'confessional' system, which divided political power between the various religious sects while ensuring Christian dominance. [10]

Under the leadership of Kamal Jumblat's Druze Progressive Socialist Party (PSP), a left-leaning and mostly Muslim group, the Lebanese National Movement (LNM) was formed to challenge this dominance and social disparity between the rich urban Christians and Muslims and the rural poor Muslims, including fishermen, in the country's south. This LNM supported the Palestinian struggle for liberation, but its focus was on Lebanese issues. Palestinians in return supported the LNM but likewise, were focused on their own liberation. In the camps that meant rising up against the oppressive regime of the Deuxieme Bureau, as the broader PLO resistance increased its attacks on Israel both from Jordan and the south of Lebanon.

These attacks came with a price as the camps that housed and hid the PLO fighters became a target for attack by the Lebanese military. I remember in particular one day in 1969 when we were evacuated

---

10 The Lebanese National Pact of 1943 is a power-sharing arrangement between Lebanese Christians and Muslims. Under the agreement the president is always a Christian, the prime minister a Sunni Muslim and the speaker of the National Assembly a Shi'a Muslim.

from school as Lebanese tanks and planes were bombing the camp and nearby area. We were all terrified: many students were injured and killed as they fled. I raced home to find that my mother had prepared all our UNRWA identification and a few clothes. She told us we were leaving the camp, as it was not safe to stay. Our house offered no protection and my mother had a cousin who lived in a block of flats just outside the camp. We ran as fast as we could to the flat while the bombing continued around us. More than 50 members of my family crowded into the two-room dwelling. My sister and brothers and I huddled together trembling in terror in the corner of the lounge room. Children cried and covered their ears to block out the sound of the bombs crashing into the buildings nearby. My mother and my aunts prayed for us to be protected from being killed.

That day two teenage brothers from my school were killed in the most brutal way. Lebanese soldiers shot and wounded one brother as he was coming into the camp near the airport road. They wounded the other brother when he ran back to save his sibling. The soldiers caught both of them and, in front of the crowd of refugees who had gathered, kicked and smashed them with their rifle butts until they died. The boys' mother, who watched this brutality helplessly from inside the camp, was traumatised for months and years from grief and shock.

The brothers were in their last year of school studying for their Baccalaureate, in preparation for going to university. I knew them well and was deeply affected by their deaths; I was too young to be able to articulate my emotions, but I became depressed and slept all the time, rarely eating. At times I would feel full of anger and want to lash out and hurt the soldiers who had killed these boys. At that time, many people I knew were being killed by bombs or were shot—but the killing of the brothers was my first contact with sense-less murder. The injustice of their deaths stays with me today.

Around this time, the father of my best friend, Salima, was also killed. During an intense attack on the camp by the Lebanese army, a shell hit Salima's house and her father was killed instantly. After that, I lived in perpetual terror of a bomb, a rocket or shell hitting our house and my family or myself being wounded or killed. Not surprisingly, I never slept deeply, always afraid something would happen. Often, when there was fighting, we had to flee the house in the night to a safe place. My mother had made a belt of cloth in which she kept our refugee papers, our birth certificates and her money. She wore it around her waist, day and night; and close at hand was always a small bag with a change of clothes for us.

When the bombing started, we would race from the house through the narrow, winding camp lanes to my cousin's place outside the camp. My brother Nader was 13, Ihab, 11, and I was nine. My sister, Hanadie, was four and my baby brother, Amer, two. One of us would carry our bag of clothes; one of the boys would take Hanadie, and my mother would carry the baby, as we ran for our lives. The men, including my father, would stay in the camp trying to protect it. It was terrifying to have this killing and death around us all the time. We children would shiver and cry, wishing we could be far away from all this noise and terror. I would think of places to which we could flee, where my family could be safe, and often it was to Tarshiha that my thoughts would travel.

While the thought of returning to Tarshiha was a momentary respite from the hell in which I lived, for my grandparents the belief they would go home never faded regardless of our circumstances. This was brought home to me in the Spring of 1970—22 years after they had been exiled at gunpoint. I was with my sisters, Mervat and Hanadie, at my grandparents' house helping my grandmother with her annual spring clean. Under my grandparents' bed I found a small box containing nails, a hammer and a large rusty key. When I saw it I asked my grandfather, Abu Ahmad, 'What's this old rusted key for?'

My grandfather answered simply, 'It is the key to our house in Palestine'.

I laughed and said with all the hurtful innocence of youth, 'What house! 'Your land is occupied. The house is not yours anymore.'

My grandfather and grandmother became very angry. Abu Ahmad grabbed the box from me, berating me. 'Don't you know what this means? This is the key to my home. This house here in this miserable camp is not my real house. My house in Palestine is the one I inherited from my parents and my grandparents and where I have fields and crops and animals. This is not my place.'

At that moment, I felt so ashamed by the hurt I had caused them—I think it was then that I truly understood at last the terrible suffering their exile caused; and a deep sorrow I could never express, lodged in my soul.

5

A PEOPLE'S ARMY

At the end of 1969, life in the camps changed dramatically. With Egyptian President Nasser brokering the talks, a PLO delegation headed by Arafat met with its Lebanese counterparts, led by General Emile Bustani. Under a deal known as the Cairo Agreement, control over the 16 Palestine refugee camps in Lebanon passed from the Lebanese Armed Forces to the Palestinian Armed Struggle Command. The Cairo Agreement essentially created a 'state within a state' and gave the PLO the authority to establish educational and humanitarian services, and under specific guidelines, to maintain a military presence in the refugee camps.[11]

It is hard to comprehend that a piece of paper could have changed our lives so much. When the PLO moved into Burj Barajneh we suddenly felt free. The hated police points around and inside our camp vanished. We could do things we could not do before. For the first time in 20 years we could build proper houses with bricks and cement, and we could build upwards to accommodate our growing families. And while our two-storey brick homes felt more able to

---

11 The *Cairo Agreement* of November 2, 1969, was an agreement between Yasser Arafat of the PLO and Lebanese army commander General Emile Bustani, brokered by the Egyptian President Gamal Abdel Nasser.

withstand any bombing raids, the PLO also built underground shelters in the camp to ensure we would have a safe place to retreat to during war.

For women like my mother, the PLO's intervention brought a revolution on the home front. It arranged for power lines from the city grid to be brought to the camp and, while we could not have power regularly, for the first time we had electric lights and could cool things in the summer. At the same time the group also increased the number of water points, tapped the artesian water under the camp, and installed pumps and water pipes. We could now wash in the mornings and women could do their housework during the day. The long nights of washing and cleaning became a thing of the past and I am sure my mother was eternally grateful to regain her sleeping hours.

These small improvements in our lives were repaid with an intense loyalty to the PLO leadership. In providing us with basic services, the PLO had reclaimed our dignity and honour, and for the first time since my family had been forced from Palestine, we felt protected. Importantly we felt we had wrested back control of our lives. Palestinians were running our government and working in our services. But as always for the Palestinians in Lebanon, this semblance of normality would be disturbed by events beyond our control.

The Cairo Agreement was strongly resisted by some of the Lebanese Christian political parties, in particular, the Christian Kata'eb party, which was backed by the Catholic Maronites. Under Pierre Gemayel, the Kata'eb, which was often referred to as the Phalangist party, had long been a paramilitary organisation with established fascist leanings. As the captain of the Lebanese football team, Gemayel had attended the 1936 Olympics in Germany and had been impressed with Hitler's National Socialism, and his youth brigades in particular. He made no secret that he was impressed by the order and discipline of Hitler's Third Reich.[12]

---

12   Fisk, R. 2002, *Pity the Nation, The Abduction of Lebanon.*

Being a major player in Lebanon's Christian community, Gemayel's Kata'eb party was ideologically opposed to the socialist-leaning LNM and its support of the Palestinians. Kata'eb also spoke against the Palestinian presence in Lebanon, not because of its socialist and pan-Arabist leanings, but for the potential threat hundreds of thousands of mostly Sunni Muslim Palestinian refugees posed to Lebanon's political 'confessional' system with its preferred treatment of Christians. As the PLO's power base grew in Lebanon, direct contact between Israel and the Christian-led Lebanese Government began to grow. The Israelis saw in Lebanon a potential ally against the Palestinians, as well as a Christian buffer against its Arab enemies who were committed to Israel's overthrow; so they began to assist and train the Christian militia.

The Christian Kata'eb party's concern over the potential for Palestinian Muslims to upset the political balance was further exacerbated by the events in Jordan. After the 1967 war with Israel, many Palestinian fighters moved to Jordan and used the Arab nation's border with Israel as a base for attacks against the occupation. As in the camps in Lebanon, Palestinians ran a state-within-a-state in Jordan, headquartered in Amman. As Arafat's organisation grew in strength, funded by a number of Arab states and Palestinians living in the Gulf who paid the PLO a portion of their salaries, the group began to openly challenge the rule of Jordan's King Hussein. The simmering conflict erupted in September 1970 when the Marxist Popular Front for the Liberation of Palestine (PFLP) hijacked four international airplanes, blowing up three in the Jordanian desert. In what is known as Black September, fighting erupted between the Jordanian military and the PLO. Thousands of Palestinian fighters and civilians living in the camps were killed as were many Jordanian civilians. This led to the expulsion of the PLO from Jordan. Many of these fighters and their families, mostly from the West Bank and Gaza, and enabled by the Cairo Agreement came to the camps in Lebanon, where they settled amongst us and received a heroes' welcome.

We were extraordinarily proud of these fighters and, with my brothers and sisters, I took any opportunity to see them training on the grounds near Haifa hospital. For me, these young men and women were the strongest people in the world. Their faces blackened with kohl, they would climb ropes, jump and crawl on the ground and run in a variety of exercises. People from the camp encouraged them, clapping furiously as each exercise was successfully completed. It was while watching our PLO military graduates train that I settled on my own career ambitions as I realised that the graduates I admired most were the men and women dressed in white—the first-aid workers. I recalled the killing of the two brothers and the death of my friend's father, and decided that, rather than be a fighter, I wanted to save lives. I would be a doctor so that I could serve my people this way.

The social and educational services the PLO provided complemented those of UNRWA. In addition to providing some preventative health clinics and emergency food, UNRWA was responsible for our education. It gave us six years in primary school and four years in high school. To get into university, we had to complete a further three years at a private school. Until the late 1960s, the content of the primary and secondary school curricula, including history and geography, was determined by UNRWA. Our Palestinian history was not part of either curriculum. But when the PLO came to the camps, that all that changed and we began to learn about our own history. This made a big difference to us as we were introduced to the ancient history of Palestine and the more recent events of 1948 that led to our exile. We were also allowed to have a student council with elected representatives whose role it was to take student concerns to teachers and the headmaster. All the Palestinian political parties were represented in the camps and at that time, in Burj Barajneh, the mainstream PLO political group was *al-Fatah*, but the Popular Front for the Liberation of Palestine, (PFLP) the Democratic Front for the Liberation of Palestine (DPLP) and the more radical group Sa'eqa also had offices there. The main political groups had women's and youth groups and most young people were involved in these groups too.

Burj Barajneh Palestinian refugee camp where Olfat and her family have spent most of their lives. Beirut, Lebanon, early 1950s.

Olfat's parents Hind and Khalil. Beirut, 1955.

Olfat aged 19 (right), with her sister Mervat. Beirut, 1979.

At home with husband Mahmoud and children, Chaker and Fayez. Burj Barajneh Palestinian refugee camp, Beirut, Lebanon, 1991.

Olfat and her mother in the tiny living room of their house. Burj Barajneh, 1999.

With her family in her current house: L-R Fayez, Olfat, Mahmoud, Hani, Hadi. Beirut, 2010.

Olfat with her sisters at her nephew's wedding: L-R Ghada, Amani, Fayez, Olfat, Helmi, Mervat, Hanadi, in front Amjad. Beirut, 2015.

Some of the bodies laid out for identification and burial after the Sabra Shatila massacre: over 2,000 Palestinians and Lebanese, including women and children, reportedly killed, 1982.

The main street of the Sabra Shatila Palestinian refugee camp, Beirut, 1983.

Bombing of Burj Barajneh on the edge of the refugee camp, 1985.

Palestinian refugee camp, Ain al Helwah in South Lebanon (housing 30,000 residents at the time) after the Israeli military campaign, 1985.

Collapsed buildings on the edge of Burj Barajneh Palestinian refugee camp after the 1985 war.

At a media conference with Cliff Dolan (President ACTU, Chair APHEDA), Olfat with four other Palestinian nurses on their first visit to Australia for community nursing training. Sydney, 1986.

Fielding a question at the same media conference in Sydney, 1986.

Bombed ov ut neighbour's house during the Amal siege of the Burj Barajneh camp, metres from Olfat's family home, 1986.

Olfat (front right) with student nurses she was teaching at the Nursing School in Bar Elias in the Beqaa Valley, 1987.

Across the globe in the 1970s many teenagers were revelling in a new-found freedom and liberty their parents had never enjoyed. Jeans were the fashion item of the moment and disco was king. But these were experiences I never shared or felt I had a right to indulge. My teenage years in the late 1970s were surrounded by war and death. All teenagers like to think they are rebels, but our rebellion was real—we were fighting to liberate Palestine.

I became involved in politics proper in 1974 with encouragement from a teacher, joining the school student council. I also began to visit the youth group's office on the camp's edge near Haifa hospital. The PLO provided us with this office space—there was a large communal area with table tennis tables and room enough for our cultural activities: singing, dancing and other performances. On the walls were posters of our leaders and martyrs. We were thirsty for knowledge and the youth group leaders often held workshops on history and politics. I learnt many administrative skills including how to work with, and co-ordinate, people. In time I also started to teach other students skills such as first aid. It was good leadership training and gave me a sense that I was helping my people, which had become very important to me.

As I became politicised I began to take more notice of world politics. I saw Arafat's 1974 address to the UN as a major breakthrough, and importantly it helped identify for me the 105 UN member states that supported our struggle for liberation. Yet it changed nothing: Israel continued in its refusal to withdraw from the Palestinian Occupied Territories and the international community remained complicit through its inaction.

The following year our world erupted as Lebanon descended into a civil war that would last 15 years. It began on an ordinary day, March 10, 1975. I was with two school friends in the centre of Beirut buying presents to mark the Lebanese National Teachers' Day[13]—a school

---

13 Teachers' Day in Lebanon is celebrated for a week from 3-9 March and is a time when children and parents can express their appreciation and gratitude to their teachers. March 9 is a holiday in most Lebanese schools.

holiday the day before—when war broke out. One minute we were shopping and laughing, the next we were surrounded by military: soldiers appeared on buildings, taking up strategic positions; tanks roared along the major roads, and fighter planes screamed overhead. Everyone around us looked at each other, their eyes wide with fear. Mothers pulled their children close, and I grasped my friends' arms for comfort. People started asking each other nervously what was happening. We became even more anxious when we saw roadblocks being erected on the main city road where we had been shopping.

People around us ran to get a bus or taxi, but none could get through the roadblocks. Along with thousands now trapped in the city, we started walking rapidly, heads down, desperate to return to the relative safety of our camp homes. Avoiding the main roads and holding each other's hands, we moved quickly through the city's back streets, passing army checkpoints and numerous military patrols. We were grateful we had our refugee cards with us otherwise we would have been arrested. Outside the centre of the city, the roads were jammed with cars, taxis and buses, all tooting their horns hoping it could somehow force the vehicle in front to move. Through all this noise and confusion, it took us more than an hour to reach our home in the camp.

Initially, the PLO steered clear of the conflict. But on 13 April when the PLO and several busloads of mourners were escorting the body of a Palestinian officer back to his family in Jordan a Christian Kata'eb militia group attacked them on the road between Beirut and Damascus. Many innocent civilians from Burj, and the Sabra and Shatila refugee camps were killed. The Palestinian military response was to take an active part in the civil war, supporting the left-wing Lebanese groups.

The initial months of conflict were marked by fierce shelling and fighting across Beirut, but it was heaviest in our part of the city. We were lucky, as we were able to leave the camp and go to my uncle's flat about two minutes walk from the camp in the Lebanese suburb of Burj el Barajneh (after which the camp was named). We sheltered

there often. During the fighting my mother, my aunt and my grandmother would stay awake all night, sitting on the mattresses on the
floor, praying together, trying to calm their fears. We would stay
close to them, huddled together for comfort; the young ones crying,
terrified by the noise of the bombing, the crashing of masonry falling
and glass shattering.

The shelling was ferocious: we were overwhelmed with the smell
of burning buildings, the dust and cordite leaving us gasping for air
and coughing, choked by the fallout. During lulls in the bombing,
we could hear the cries of people in the nearby flats. Relatives and
many young people I knew were killed. One neighbour was blown
to pieces in their home, another left the camp and never returned.

It was a terrifying time and I began to have vivid, horrifying
dreams. I could not eat. I would think of these young people, of
the happy times we had had together, and I would be filled with
an overwhelming sense of sadness and loss. But at the same time, I
would feel a fury and frustation that we were trapped in someone
else's war. It was confusing and incomprehensible. We as Palestinians did not fight each other because of religion. Christian and Muslim Palestinians fought side by side to liberate Palestine and I could
not understand why in Lebanon there was so much hatred.

While we would wait in the flat for a lull in the bombing, my
grandmother would remind us that people were not always divided
by religion. She would point to the example of the refugees from
Tarshiha who rejected attempts by the Lebanese government to
separate them along religious lines in the camp. She talked of the
experience of her Christian friend, Miriam, from the Palestinian
village of Safid. When they had fled the Israeli attacks with their
Muslim and Christian neighbours, they had to resist efforts to separate them, rejecting offers of Lebanese nationality for the Christian
members of their village. The UN even constructed a special camp
for Palestinian Christians in East Beirut called Dbeyeh and another
one in West Beirut called Mar Elias. But the religious lines of these
camps were soon broken as Muslims moved into the camps because

they wanted to be with friends from their own villages, irrespective of their religion.

By September 1975, Lebanon was effectively split into two major cantons. In fierce fighting the leftist, mostly secular, LMN had gained dominance in West Beirut and the south of Lebanon, while the Christians were dominant in East Beirut and in some parts of the north. Kata'eb head, Bashir Gemayel, formed a new and expanded militia alliance: the Christian Lebanese Forces. Israel provided increasing aid training and military support to this group. But nothing is ever simple in Lebanon and in early 1976, trying to avert a complete collapse, the weakened Lebanese National Parliament asked Syria for military help. Its armed forces were to stay in Lebanon for the next 30 years.[14] The war quickly escalated and soon Christian militia in East Beirut started to 'ethnically cleanse' the area of Muslims, mostly Shi'a, who fled to the slums of West Beirut. The Palestinians in the refugee camps in East Beirut were targeted as well, but unlike the Shi'a, they were not allowed to escape.

The UN camp of Tel al-Za'atar (Hill of Thyme) was inhabited predominantly by Muslim refugees who came from an area in Palestine called Ghoor. Their skin was dark and the women were tattooed on their chins and faces much as Palestinian Bedouins do. They, like all the Palestinians, tried to stay together as a community; the camp housed around 30,000 refugees as well as many impoverished Lebanese from the south, mostly Shi'a Muslims. Internally and on the periphery, the camp was protected by the PLO, but the Kata'eb was dominant in the district. On 4 January 1976, the Christian Lebanese Forces surrounded and sealed the camp. No one could enter or leave, not even UNRWA or the local or International Committee of the Red Cross.

---

14 The Syrian Army entered Lebanon in June 1976. Its presence was legitimised in October that year by the League of Arab States through the formation of the Arab Deterrent Force. Of 30,000 troops, 27,000 were Syrian—Rabil, R, *From Beirut to Algiers: The Arab League's role in the Lebanon Crisis*, Washington Institute, Policywatch 976.

In the seven-month siege of Tel al-Za'atar that followed, more than 2,500 people died in the fighting or from injuries. Thousands were wounded and thousands more disappeared. On 11 August alone more than 1,500 unarmed civilians—women, children and old men— from the camp were executed by the Kata'eb as they tried to walk to safety. By the time the siege was over a camp that had housed more than 30,000 UN-protected refugees had been erased. [15]

I was 15 years old and I can remember the events as if they took place yesterday. The survivors were brought to Sports City Stadium in Beirut where Palestinians from across Lebanon, myself included, came to help them. The stories I heard as I spoke with survivors are imprinted on my soul. I wept that day and my heart felt as if it was shattering into pieces as I tried to absorb the horrors these people had endured. Many Palestinians had relatives in Tel al-Za'atar and people from all over Beirut, outside and inside the refugee camps, opened their houses for the survivors.

In our camp my neighbour was looking after Umm Afeef, a widow in her late sixties who had lost three children and a son-in-law in the massacre, and was looking after her daughter's baby girl. Although strongly believing in her faith, Umm Afeef would say over and over, 'How could God let this happen? There is no God in this world.' My mother would sit with her and calm her; and call on God to give Umm Afeef the strength to live with her great loss. This gentle understanding and the quiet prayers of my mother, would cause this poor woman to burst into tears, crying and wailing with uncontrollable grief.

There were many eyewitness accounts but one that is etched in my mind is the brutal killing of a 10-year-old boy. His mother, a survivor herself, told me the story. She had lost all her sons in the massacre and the last was this child. The mother was with a large group of people who had gathered together in preparation to leave the camp. The right-wing Christian parties who had attacked the

15 Cobban, Helena. 1984, *The Palestinian Liberation Organisation: People, Power, and Politics*, Cambridge University Press, p. 142.

camp stopped this group and arbitrarily singled out this woman and her son. She pleaded with them, 'Please, do not harm him. He is the last boy I have. Please, do not harm him.' They said, 'No, no just sit down. We are not going to harm him. We are not going to do anything to him.' They put the boy in her lap as if to let him sleep, and then they shot him in the head right there, on her lap.

After this, the mother, like many of these women, became severely mentally disturbed. How could they remain sane? In time, with the loving support of women such as my mother, she recovered as best as she could and lived amongst us with her remaining family, in Burj Barajneh camp.

Another woman who survived these war crimes became mute after witnessing the brutal killing of her brother. He was killed at one of the Kata'eb checkpoints. When the siblings approached the militia they asked the boy, 'What are you eating?'

When he replied, 'I am eating nothing', one of them pushed his cheek with a small pistol, saying, 'No, no, you are eating something. You are chewing something.'

Her brother again said, 'No there is nothing there. I am not eating.'

The soldier said to him, 'Okay, open your mouth so I can see'.

The minute her brother did as he was asked, the soldier shot him in the mouth, as his sister looked on frozen in horror. In her extreme shock, this poor woman was never able to speak again. She too settled in our camp, and later worked as a cleaner at Haifa hospital.

While these events affected me deeply and were profoundly horrifying, they actually made me stronger in my determination not to abandon my people, but to fight, to make a contribution in the best way I could.

6

NURSING THE ENEMY

My second last year of high school, 1978, would turn out to be a pivotal one—personally and politically.

The Arab-Israeli conflict moved to a new phase in March when Israel invaded Lebanon for the second time in a massive ground and air assault. More than 25,000 troops occupied the country to the Letani River, in what was called the Bridges War. More than 2,000 Lebanese civilians were killed, and more than 200,000 people, most of them Shi'a Muslims fled, as Israeli bombs and rockets destroyed their villages along with roads, bridges, wells, and water and electricity infrastructure. The displaced residents from southern Lebanon swelled the slums in West Beirut, creating even more conflict.

At the international level, the UN passed Resolution 425, calling for a ceasefire and an Israeli withdrawal from the south of Lebanon, and deploying 6,000 UN troops along the border of a 10-kilometre buffer zone to monitor the peace. But Israel, in effect, remained in control of this southern zone by handing over control of this border strip to its proxy South Lebanon Army, made up of Christian militia. Its role was to keep the PLO and its Lebanese supporters away from Israeli settlements.

Through its invasion, Israel had created a small Christian canton on its border, but its support of Lebanon's Christian community did not end there. When Christian forces clashed with Syrian troops in East Beirut, Israeli military jets screamed over Beirut, skimming the tops of the buildings in the seaside area of Corniche Mazraa, terrifying the city's residents; while Israeli gunboats simultaneously shelled West Beirut in support of their Christian allies. By the end of 1978, the Syrian-led Arab Deterrent Force was forced out of East Beirut and this section of the city and the surrounding mountain came under the full military control of Christian forces, armed and trained by the Israelis. The country was by now divided with Beirut split along the so-called Green Line. In the east were the Christian Lebanese Forces, supported regionally by the Israelis and internationally by the US. West Beirut was under the control of the Muslim-dominated LNM, supported by most Arab nations and internationally by the USSR.

Throughout that year, the war was an everyday part of my life. I never slept without hearing the sound of shooting, shelling and bombing. But 1978 was also the year I met the man who would later become my husband, Mahmoud Khazaal. We were studying at the same school and Mahmoud, a determined young man, was agitating for the students to hold a demonstration against Israel's invasion. Mahmoud's older brother had been killed when Israel had invaded, along with many other Palestinians and Lebanese fighting in south Lebanon. Even before his brother died, however, Mahmoud had been urging all the students at our high school, run by UNRWA just outside the camp, to express their anger by boycotting classes and going on strike. When the bell rang at the start of the day, we normally had to stand in a row before filing into class.

One day, we all agreed that we would refuse to go into our classrooms. The school director came around and began to threaten us with expulsion, so eventually most of the students caved in. With some others, Mahmoud included, I refused to go inside. Because I had been a model student and was top of my class, the school director approached me and said he was surprised by my actions.

'I must keep my word when we all have an agreement, and you should not encourage us to break our word,' I told him. 'We supported Mahmoud's suggestion to boycott classes and we should all take responsibility for that agreement. If you want to build a good generation of people, you should respect our views and ideals. Because of this I will not leave those whom I have supported.'

The director agreed that there was logic in my argument but said that he did not want us to miss our studies. I replied that our feelings about our people were important too. So, we maintained our strike, which is how I met Mahmoud.

The war and cultural considerations meant our social life as teenagers was quite circumscribed. Going into the centre of Beirut to the cinema or other public places was out of the question as they were often targets for car bombers. Also, in our culture girls and boys did not mix socially in the way that western teenagers do, rarely spending time alone together. So Mahmoud and I spent our time with our friends in a group situation. We looked on boys as our comrades and concentrated on doing various things to improve camp life and to care for our family and friends there. I was attracted to boys because of their work for our cause and our community; and by their honesty, punctuality and energy. It was all of these qualities that attracted me to Mahmoud, although his good looks added to the attraction. At our student strike he had demonstrated that he wanted to do something for our people and was prepared to face the consequences of these actions. But the line between propriety and intimacy was never crossed. Love was not sexual or romantic; it was more a caring, worrying and fear of loss. Our greatest concern was that the person we cared for would die. This fear overwhelmed any sexual or romantic feelings. So, our lives were centred in the camp, at school and in our struggle to liberate Palestine.

In Burj Barajneh and at school, I continued with my various student activities. We produced newsletters, displayed articles on the walls, undertook various cultural activities such as traditional dancing, and held workshops on traditional Palestinian embroidery. My sisters and I were so skilled in this last craft that we actually made quite lot of money by selling various items. This enabled us to help with the household budget as well as have some pocket money. Like many others, my father had lost his job at the start of the civil war as his work had been in the Christian sector in East Beirut, so our embroidery became an important source of income for my family.

Of course, all the Palestinian political parties were active in the camp, and many of them were recruiting young people for their political work. At one point, a woman who belonged to al-Fatah, came to our student group and started to run courses on politics. I liked the way this woman was teaching, so I joined, but only for a few weeks as I was not happy to do things without informing my parents. They were not against me being involved in student politics, but they wanted me to put my studies first. They would say that when I was an adult, I would be able to make the right decision about which political group I wanted to actively support. At the same time, we would talk openly about the situation with my parents, our neighbours, our friends and our teachers. We felt that politics was like bread and we needed to have it every day. But at that time, I agreed with my parents—it was too early for me to be involved in a political party.

Nonetheless, when the fighting stopped towards the end of 1978, and the city was divided into West and East Beirut, I could not help but get caught up in the political developments in the camp. I started to talk with Mahmoud and the rest of the students and began to deepen my understanding of Zionism and the role this ideology was playing in Palestine. The boys in the camp and Mahmoud too were politically active in their support for the PLO, attending meetings, discussing the situation in the south of Lebanon, developments within the PLO and the need for international support.

During these years we students supported the PLO's attempts to bring our cause to the attention of the international community. Leila Khaled was a member of a group called the Palestinians for the Liberation of Palestine (PFLP), whose members were involved in hijacking planes. As a teenager I was very proud of her. We all felt the world should know about our situation, and her actions were giving our plight global attention. Unlike other hijackings later, those Leila were involved in did not result in deaths. The people she hijacked were released, all unharmed, and while they caused international outrage, we felt the actions of these militants were totally justified—yes, those planes were not ours, and our actions were illegal and against international rules and laws. But the same argument applied to the Palestinian territories—the Israelis had stolen our lands and their actions were illegal under international law. So where was the outrage for Palestinians at that time? Our people had lived in misery in camps for decades, and had been killed and massacred in thousands—and the world was shocked when we took action?

I always ask people what they would do if someone kicked them out of their house and said, 'Sorry this is not your home. You must leave.' Of course, that person would be furious. In most countries there are laws to protect people's possessions, but Palestinians have had their entire lives stolen; and all the international laws that should protect us and give us our rights are ignored. As a result, millions of us have existed in miserable camps for decades. What are we expected to do? Are we expected to be silent and just slide into more poverty and despair? I was young, but I could see this was not fair; and inevitably, the injustice of our position fired my revolutionary spirit. As a teenager, I supported the hijacking of planes and I think if someone had asked me to help with a hijacking at that time I would have done so. I was so angry at all the things I had witnessed that I was ready to sacrifice my own life to liberate Palestine.

As these events raged around me, I graduated from school in 1979 with excellent results. Although I had dreamed of studying medicine for many years, I knew my father would not be able to support me financially to study in Lebanon. I confidently applied to the PLO for a scholarship to study in Russia or Bulgaria, translating all of my papers into English and copying my academic transcript. I took them to the relevant PLO office, going back each week, to see if they had any news. At the same time staff at the office were telling me to come back the following week for news, other students were already being awarded their scholarships and starting to leave the country.

In time I realised I would not be getting a scholarship—not because I didn't deserve one, but because I did not have a *waasta* or backer. I had assumed that scholarships were awarded solely on the basis of our school reports, but it turned out to be much more political than that. My family were not active members of the PLO and I had only been active in school council activities, and so we had no political connections as such. We were ordinary Palestinians and we were committed to our country, but we were not active in any of the PLO parties.

Once I realised what the situation was, I was determined my father would not see how bitterly disappointed I was. He was already extremely upset because he could not support my studies. I didn't want to humiliate him even more by showing how it was affecting me. So, I gave my family many excuses as to why I did not get a scholarship, but inside, I was burning with anger at this injustice, and felt deeply distressed that a movement I supported was based on such unfair principles. I remembered the joy I had experienced at my opportunity to vote in the student elections and the exhilaration of having elected a student body that was representative and democratic. But after seeing how scholarship selections were made, I felt as if the PLO leaders had betrayed all of us who had supported and believed in them.

With medicine off the radar, I turned my ambitions towards nursing and, with the help of some Palestinian doctors at Haifa hospital who I knew in Burj Barajneh camp, was admitted to the Palestinian Red Crescent Society (PRCS) Nursing School, based at Aka hospital, located on the edge of Sabra and Shatila refugee camps in Beirut. I started my three-year general nursing training in October 1979 with a three-month block of nursing theory, before moving to Gaza hospital, which also overlooked the Sabra and Shatila refugee camps.

Frances Moore, the wife of the First Secretary at the British Embassy in Lebanon, was our main teacher but there were local teachers as well. I respected Mrs Moore—who was a volunteer with Unipal (Universities' Trust for Educational Exchange with Palestinians)—a great deal and, as my English was good and she could not speak Arabic, I translated for her in class. When we went to do practical experience in the hospital, we had to complete work plans. Later, Mrs Moore and I would sit together while I translated the other students' work for her. When translating in class, I had to listen very closely, so I actually learnt my lessons twice. I particularly loved doing my nursing experience in the hospital, often working well after my shift had finished. The more experience I had, the more I enjoyed, and knew for sure that I was in the right career.

One day in July 1980, Mahmoud Agha, the head nurse at Gaza hospital, came to the surgical ward where I was working and asked me to follow him to the second floor. I was curious, as I knew that floor was normally used as a storage area. Following him into one of the big rooms, I was astonished to see it full of young men in hospital beds with serious leg, arm and head wounds. There was no fighting near our area at that time, but we knew the Christian groups were fighting each other.

'What is this? Who are all these wounded men?' I asked.

He was evasive. 'I want you to help me and be responsible for the care of these men,' he said.

I was in my first year of nursing but by then had had a lot of experience, and I was open-minded about many things. I quickly discovered they were not Palestinians but from one of the Lebanese right-wing groups. Most of the time the predominantly Christian right-wing paramilitary groups fought for territory and control over areas of Beirut and Lebanon against the leftist LNM. But from time to time, in what appeared totally senseless to all of us, these Christian militia—the Kata'eb, dominated by the Gemayel family, or Chamoun's militia, the Al Ahrar—fought each other.

So, it was on this day and for whatever political reason, Arafat had ordered the wounded members of the Al Ahrar militia be brought to the hospital where I worked. But, I remember thinking,

these were members of the militias that had murdered my country-
men in Tel al-Za'atar; to have them there in the hospital filled me
with anger. Agha could sense my rage and tried to calm me. 'I know
you respect people as human beings, irrespective of their religion.'

'Yes, I do', I replied. 'But you know also that to bring them here
endangers their lives. What if some Palestinians hear that they're
here and come and attack them. Why was this decision taken?'

'It is not my decision,' Agha told me, 'but Arafat's and his brother
Fathe's, as head of the Palestinian Red Crescent Society (PRCS).
They gave the order to admit them to the hospital and I have to obey
orders. So now I want you to work here with them.'

I remember those soldiers and that day, clearly. They were all
young boys in their late teens or early twenties, initially eight or nine
of them. Later, more were brought in. Several doctors were with
me and another nurse. The young men were very soiled, bloodied
and wounded so we cleaned their wounds, covered them and then
helped them to wash. We also offered them food, but they said they
had eaten. In the evening we offered them food again, and again,
they said no.

So I asked, 'At lunch you did not eat and now it is night and you
are still not eating. Is there a problem?'

'There is no problem, we are just not hungry,' one of them replied.

It was then I realised they did not trust us.

'I'll show you that the food is safe. Choose any tray of food that
you like, and I'll eat from that tray,' I said to them.

They looked at each other and, after apologising, started to eat.
And they were indeed very hungry. While they ate, we started to
talk. One of them said to me, 'We want to see Palestinians'.

'You have been seeing Palestinians all day long! What's wrong
with you? I am Palestinian, Dr Khalid, Dr Abid and all the body-
guards who are protecting you are Palestinians—all except Dr
Yarno—he is from Canada.'

'No, no,' they said, 'We want to see real Palestinians.'

I laughed and said, 'We *are* real Palestinians,' and I brought my refugee papers to show them. They were all looking at my card and then at me.

Then one of them, a young boy, said, 'But we were told that you are not like human beings. We were told that you are not civilised, that you are like monsters in a way, with long nails.'

I looked at him, appalled: 'Who told you this? We are human beings like everyone else. We have pale-skinned people and we have very dark Palestinians, and some of our people are rich while others are very poor. We have Christians and Muslims too. We are a nation like all nations, just like everyone else. Look at Lebanon, you too have Bedouin who have green marks on their faces. You, too, have people with different accents—look at the accent from Balbek. You, too, have people who are very dark, and you have Christians and Muslims. Why is it that Lebanese only think of themselves as Christian or Muslim instead of a nation with different religions and different-coloured people?'

This boy looked at me and said, 'You are right.'

'Yes, this is the problem we Palestinians have had in our lives. You look at us as if we are not human beings when we are just like you,' I replied, shocked by what he had said. Yet his beliefs explained so much of our experience as refugees in this country that had never accepted us as citizens or as having rights of any kind.

Another nurse and I worked in that place for more than a week. These young men wanted to see Sabra and Shatila, as they had heard a lot about the camp. We were on the second floor of the hospital and when we took them to the balcony they could see over the camp. They were only young boys and they regretted being involved in war. Like all of us, they wanted a normal, peaceful life. One day their leader, Chamoun, came to the hospital to see them. Protected by the PLO guards, Chamoun gave the boys money and asked them if they were happy. He thanked us for looking after them and then left. I felt angry inside, as he had given the orders to slaughter our people so brutally in Tel al-Za'atar. But at this particular moment in their fight against the Kata'eb, Chamoun was being supported and protected by the Lebanese left-wing groups and the PLO. It seemed to me that a kind of madness reigned in Lebanon. Nothing made sense. By contrast our own struggle was based on a clear and simple premise, the liberation of Palestine, and we were united in this one objective.

A few months after these young men had left the hospital, I met one of them at Aka Hospital. He told me he'd left Chamoun's militia and was working in a local shop. He said that many of the boys had left and some had left Lebanon altogether. I felt I had played a role in these decisions by showing them that people are the same regardless of where we come from. I was so happy to have made the decision to become a nurse—I felt I was playing a very important role for our cause in more ways than one.

7

ENCIRCLED

From 1979 to the middle of 1981, we were relatively safe and free from war with the LNM and Syrian troops controlling West Beirut. There was conflict on the Green Line and clashes between the various Christian Lebanese Forces' groups, but these did not involve us. But while the times were relatively peaceful, there was still no peace. We knew Israel wanted the PLO destroyed, and even though the ceasefire held along the South Lebanese border, we were waiting and preparing for more war.

Events in Lebanon as well as in the region were certainly pointing to more conflict. In the south of the country and in the southern suburbs of West Beirut—in the area where my camp was—some of the impoverished Shi'a Lebanese community were beginning to mobilise around a nationalist secular resistance movement called Amal, headed by Nabih Berri. Many of the Shi'a living in the city had been displaced from South Lebanon. While they initially supported the PLO and the LNM in the struggle for Palestinian liberation, they turned against both movements when the price of their support was the loss of their homes and villages. During March 1980, there were clashes between Amal and the PLO and the LNM in West Beirut, but the latter forces were too strong militarily. At the same time there were serious clashes in East Beirut between various groups that formed the Christian Lebanese Forces alliance. Bashir Gemayel eliminated Chamoun's militia, Al Ahrar, from East Beirut. The Christian Kata'eb was now the dominant military and political group within the Lebanese forces, backed and armed by Israel. Regional and international interests again fuelled Lebanon's internal struggle for power.

At the regional level, in September 1980, Iraq, supported by the US and other western countries, invaded Iran at the start of a disastrous eight-year war. The PLO, a long-time supporter of Iraq, was asked by Iranian leader, Ayatollah Khomeini, to support the predominantly Shi'a Iran. When the PLO refused, PLO relations with the Shi'a community in Lebanon soured considerably. Then in March 1981, Syria, supported by the Soviet Union, placed several SAM-6 missile batteries in strategic locations in the Beqaa Valley. Israel objected to this move and the US was called in to mediate even though it was Israel's major arms supplier and backer. Three months later in July, Israel bombed West Beirut for the first time since 1974, and supported Gemayel in his run for the position of Lebanon's president. In the south, the Shi'a began to turn against the PLO and started to co-operate with the South Lebanon Army in the Israeli-controlled buffer zone. Lebanon was awash with intrigue and counter-intrigue in a deadly game of international, regional and local power play. Palestinians in the camps, including my family and I, naturally feared the worst.

The bombing of West Beirut by the Israelis in 1981 hailed the end of our short respite from war. There was heavy bombing around Aka Hospital near the Sabra and Shatila camps and Christian Lebanese Forces positioned nearby on the Green Line also attacked us. We were expecting a serious war with Israel, and Arafat called students home from overseas to help the PLO. Many returned from Russia, Bulgaria and the Gulf to undertake military training. Fighting between the PLO with its supporters in the south, and Israel continued, but Israel had a bolder mission in mind and, with its Christian allies, was preparing for a full-scale assault on West Beirut.

Like the other nurses and doctors, throughout the war, I worked day and night in the hospital, rarely going home to rest—I felt deeply that it was my duty to care for my people. Even though I was young and relatively inexperienced in nursing (I was still only in my second year of training), I was often in charge of a whole ward. Student nurses were sent to the various PRCS hospitals in Beirut to get more practical experience. In Gaza Hospital I worked in the surgical and emergency wards. I did not like medical or children's wards as I found the children's pain and suffering too distressing. I had some operating-room experience, but in 1980 and 1981 most of my experience was in the surgical ward.

During the clashes, UNRWA schools were closed and the students were sent to their homes in the camps. On the journey from one of the schools to the camp, several children from one family—the Dabdoubs—were killed and others injured. One of those injured was a 10-year-old girl who had an abdominal wound and needed a laparotomy and a blood transfusion. Her blood group was the very rare B negative. Dr Hala, then a student doctor who'd come back from Russia, and I, decided to travel to nearby military bases to find someone with the correct blood type. With a driver and a blood-testing kit, we left in the afternoon and, under heavy shelling, went to many of the military bases in Beirut and even to the students who had come for military training, explaining the situation to all these people. Some knew their blood group, but we tested many others until we found four people with the right blood type. It was midnight by the time we returned to the hospital with these four donors. The operation was performed on the little girl that night, the doctors removing bullets and shrapnel from her abdomen. She was given a temporary colostomy, and with the necessary blood transfusion, this little girl's life was saved. I nursed her post-operatively and it was so satisfying to see her make a full recovery. Because she had lost a brother and sister, her parents were deeply grateful for what everyone in the hospital had done for her.

One day around this same time, during a ceasefire, I went home for a break. It was some distance to our house, so I took a *service,* a type of communal taxi. Just as I was about to return to work, heavy fighting broke out again.

My aunt said, 'Where are you going? You can't leave now.'

I replied, 'Don't you remember that I am a nurse and I have to be at the hospital.'

My aunt said in anguish, 'You can't get to the hospital. Other nurses there will take your shift.'

But I said, 'No, no, I have to go. God will protect me.'

I left and searched in vain for a *service.* The streets were deserted, so I decided to walk. The shelling and firing was very heavy. I walked through the narrow, back lanes from my camp to the main road, hugging the sides of the buildings all the way. I could hear the shelling to my right in the Ghobeiry area. I could hear bullets hitting buildings. I was walking under the Ghobeiry Bridge when a man I didn't know jumped from the corner of the bridge and pushed me to the wall.

He shouted at me, 'Are you crazy. Can't you see that there's fighting everywhere!'

I said to him, 'Why are you here?'

He replied, 'Because I am a fighter.'

'But I am a nurse and when you get wounded I will care for you. I have to get to the hospital.'

'Okay, you are a nurse, but I will walk with you.'

'Why?' I replied. 'If something happens, two of us will be wounded or killed. No, I can manage by myself. Thank you.'

So, I walked on alone. Now the fighting was on either side of the road where I was walking. A building near me was hit by a shell and my heart leapt but, somehow, I felt I would be safe ... it was an odd feeling. I was covered with dust and I had no choice but to keep going to the hospital. I was dressed not in my nurse's uniform but in ordinary clothes. I had make-up on, my hair was done and I was wearing shoes with heels. I had been expecting to travel by *service.* Whenever

I wore heels I would waddle a bit like a duck. When I arrived at the hospital I was covered with dust and could hardly see from the grit in my eyes. The nurses and doctors looked me up and down and said, 'What! No wounds? No bullets? How come? There's heavy bombing and shelling and yet you are not injured?'

No one believed I could walk from the camp to the hospital through all that heavy fighting without getting hurt or killed. One of the nurses with a good sense of humour made a joke that I had survived because instead of walking straight I had waddled from side to side and so every time a soldier had me in his sights I would move to the left or right! With that, we all laughed until we cried.

It may seem strange, but in situations like this I have never really been afraid. I have always believed I will die when the time is right and that could even be when I'm in a shelter. My real fear has been to lose someone I love rather than being wounded or killed myself.

Nurses and health workers all over the world have to deal with, at times horrific things, but in a war zone, it is on a daily basis. There was one patient I will never forget. He was a large man in his early twenties, whose face had been badly burned leaving him blind in both eyes. When he had recovered consciousness, we gently told him what had happened, but as his eyes were bandaged, he did not accept that his sight was gone. When the bandages were taken off and he realised he couldn't see, he became angry, lashing out, and smashing everything around him. I could understand his reaction completely. Apart from losing this most essential faculty, in Lebanon he faced a future that offered little support for people with disabilities.

On another occasion, a university student was brought to the hospital from the Green Line. This young man was not in a military uniform, so he was not a fighter, but his body had more than 45 bullet holes—it looked like a strainer. I was wrapping him in white sheets ready for the mortuary when one of our X-ray technicians came in.

'Olfat, how can you cope with this? Aren't you frightened by this sight?' he asked.

'What can I do. Somehow, we all have to cope with this horror. This boy is someone's son, and I have to look after him now,' I replied.

During that period, several nurses and I formed a non-formal nurse's association. This meant I was active in organising a number of social events, including one for International Nurses' Day on May 12. We also had a role in liaising between the student nurses and the Board of the School of Nursing. For instance, if there was a problem with any of the students, we would set up a meeting between the School Board, our association and the student, effectively advocating for the students, taking their concerns to the Board.

Once we organised a trip to the south of Lebanon to visit fighters at Arnoun near the border with Israel. It was a deserted and barren area even though we had passed fields of orchards on our way. When we told the fighters we were student nurses they suggested that in times of conflict the PRCS should work more in these forward areas to provide immediate medical support to the wounded. We really felt for these young men: it was very cold and they were living in tents in a difficult and dangerous situation. We stayed on over lunch and tea to give them a bit of moral support. I couldn't help feeling proud of these men and women who were prepared to give their lives so that we could return home. It is not easy to leave your family and come and live under such conditions knowing a major conflict can start any time. We were all playing a waiting game.

Our waiting ended on June 3, 1982 when there was an assassination attempt on Shlomo Argov, the Israeli ambassador to Britain,[16] by the radical Palestinian—but anti-PLO—terrorist group, Abu Nidal. Using this as a pretext, even though the ceasefire still held and was monitored by the United Nations Interim Force in Lebanon (UNIFIL), on June 6, Israel invaded Lebanon for the second time in four years. In the Beqaa Valley, the Israeli air strikes destroyed many of the Syrian SAM-6 bases and, with its vastly superior military force,

---

16 Shlomo Argov, Obituary, *The Guardian* newspaper, February 25, 2003. https://www. theguardian.com/world/2003/feb/25/israelandthepalestinians.lebanon.

overran what little opposition there was in the south. The war every-one had been expecting and fearing had begun.

I was in my last year of nurses training when the invasion started and was preparing to take my final exams. Mindful of the requests made to us by our young fighters in the south, I and a number of other student nurses went to the PRCS and suggested we work as first-aid workers and nurses in the ambulances.

On June 9, my friend Nadia and I were sent with an ambulance and its driver to collect a fighter with a serious head injury in the Damour area, just south of the beachside tourist town of Khaldeh, about 20 minutes from our hospital. The road was empty of any civilian traffic, but there was no fighting. Having experienced years of civil war in Lebanon, we were used to a heavy military presence and we could feel the tension in our fighters as we passed through the numerous checkpoints. We came to a PRCS first-aid post and our fighters told us to advance with care. Everyone was on high alert and our pulses, too, were racing.

As we advanced further, we were exhorted again to be espe-cially careful as everyone we passed was expecting aerial bombing in Khaldeh at any time. When we heard this, Nadia and I looked at each other and in unison said our Islamic prayer of protection. Af-ter going through Khaldeh, we continued on to Damour where we picked up an injured solider who was bleeding profusely, the ban-dage around his head soaked through with blood. His breathing was laboured, and he was unconscious; we knew we had to get him back to the hospital as quickly as possible. We redressed his wound and positioned him so as to assist his breathing. There was no oxygen or other resuscitation equipment in the ambulance; we did our best to make him comfortable and began the journey back to Beirut.

Then, as expected, the Israeli planes started to bomb. We tried to enter Damour but realised to our horror the Israeli tanks and armoured vehicles had advanced there already. We were trapped. We could not go back to Khaldeh or forward. Frantically, we discussed with the ambulance driver all the possible routes we could use to escape being killed or worse, taken prisoner. We looked for the small road we knew would take us off the seaboard highway, away from the fighting on the narrow coastal strip, to the mountainous area of Lebanon controlled by the Druze. But we were not sure how far the Israeli army had advanced into the mountains either, so were relieved when we came across the Druze military checkpoints and knew for the moment we were safe. However, our patient slipped into a deeper coma and was struggling for his life.

Anxious to be well away from the army advancing up the coast, we drove rapidly through the narrow and dangerous mountain roads until eventually we reached the main road that led up through the Shouf mountains towards the scenic town of Aley, overlooking Beirut. The journey took hours, along a potholed, mostly gravel road that cut a wide semi-circle high through the mountains back towards Beirut. It was summer, and although it was cooler up there than on the coast, we were hot, thirsty and exhausted. We could do nothing for our patient. I sat in the back with him as he fought for his life.

We passed easily through many Druze military checkpoints and, as they were supporting the Lebanese National Movement (LNM) and the Palestinians, they barely looked at our papers. We could see that they, too, were on high alert and very tense. When we reached Aley it was quiet and peaceful—as if the calm before a storm. We drove straight to the local hospital, but by then our patient had died. I was filled with a despair and deep, deep sadness. Countless memories of other losses flashed through my mind—another one of our people gone, another funeral, another loved father or brother or uncle lost. More families to grieve and mourn. I said a prayer for him, covered him respectfully and, helped by the nurses in the hospital, took his body to the morgue. We left the hospital and searched for the PLO's Al-Fatah office in the town. When we found it a young man opened the door.

'Who are you? What do you want?' he asked.

'We're from the PRCS in Beirut,' I replied.

I explained what had happened and that we needed to radio the PRCS in Beirut. I asked to see the base leader, only to be told he had already left. Looking at the young soldiers before me, my heart sank—I feared for them as much as for ourselves. We had heard the Israeli army had already entered the Beqaa Valley and we were fairly certain they would advance on Aley from there. In spite of their tension and anxiety, these young Palestinian soldiers were hospitable. We could not contact Beirut, but they insisted on preparing food for us—fried potato chips, labneh and bread—which we washed down with sweet black tea. Afterwards, realising that it would be impossible to travel through the night, we lay down on the floor to rest, sleeping only fitfully for a few hours—we were terrified that after all our effort getting this far, we might be trapped there.

In the morning we tried to leave the town. We knew the area was generally friendly; the Druze militia controlled the mountains through the Shouf, and the Syrian army was in the Beqaa Valley and controlled the highway from the mountains to Beirut. We knew also that both the Lebanese leftist forces and the PLO were in bases in these areas as well. With the driver and the two of us crammed into the front of the ambulance, we headed out of town to the main highway that led down the mountain towards Beirut. Just outside Aley, we stopped at a Syrian military checkpoint and a young officer told us we could not go on as Israeli planes were bombing the road ahead.

'If you go that way you will surely be killed. The Israelis are landing soldiers from helicopters and killing many people,' he said. We were in a Palestinian ambulance clearly marked with the internationally recognised Red Crescent (the Arab equivalent of the Red Cross) and knew from experience that nurses and ambulance drivers were no safer than anyone else. In times of war, we were supposed to be protected under the UN Geneva Convention, but we were not. We discussed turning back and taking the main highway to Chtaura in the Beqaa Valley. But the officer interrupted, 'The road to Chtaura is also being bombed by Israeli planes and is much too dangerous for you. Go back to Aley and see if you can leave by another route.'

With the Israelis advancing from the coast, up through the mountains to Aley and bombing the main road to Damascus, we were encircled. The driver turned the ambulance around and we headed back to Aley. The PRCS hospital in Beirut seemed an eternity away. But as we were driving and discussing our dilemma, the Israeli forces began attacking Aley; we could see dust and smoke rising as gunfire from helicopters circling above hit the far side of the town. We could also hear the thud of heavy tank shells. We drove on undeterred, and once in the town, we raced to the local hospital knowing an ambulance would be needed. The doctors immediately directed us to Kabrishmoun, a square in the town centre, to pick up casualties. When we arrived, Nadia, the driver and I jumped out, then stopped in our tracks. In front of us was a scene of hellish carnage. I felt as if I were walking through the set of a horror movie. It was unreal. There was an eerie silence. Smoke was rising from burnt-out tanks and there were bodies, contorted and mangled, amid smouldering wreckage. The entire square was filled with a mass of dead and dying humanity. I was sickened by the scene; yet frozen with fear.

We learned later that all the young men in this square were Palestinian volunteers from Jordan. An officer had been with them doing military exercises when the Israeli army attacked, bombing and killing all of them.

We were brought back to our senses by Palestinian fighters calling to us from the other side of the square.

'Leave the area immediately!' they yelled. 'The Israelis are nearby. You are in great danger. Look, on the hill behind you.'

We turned and clearly saw on a nearby hill several Israeli tanks, their guns pointed at the square. My heart, already racing, beat even faster. My throat tightened and, my mouth was suddenly dry—I couldn't swallow. My knees weakened as I struggled to control my rising terror. I was dressed in my white nurse's uniform and the ambulance was clearly marked as well. But I had no refugee identity card. When we left the hospital in Beirut, we were on duty and, of course, we had left our bags with our refugee papers at the hospital.

I turned to Nadia. 'What if we are caught and taken prisoner? Will they believe we are nurses?' I asked, pleading.

Then over the loudspeakers we heard the Israelis say in Arabic, 'Leave this area immediately. Do not fight us. Let us advance peacefully. We will kill you if you fight back.'

Suddenly, as if waking from a nightmare, I realised we had to do something. With our uniforms and ambulance, we were clearly medical workers, and we wanted to check if any of these poor men lying there were alive. At that point I heard a groan of pain. A short distance from the ambulance a Palestinian officer lay sprawled across several dead bodies. I could see that his arm was lying at an odd angle—it had been almost severed near the elbow. He had many other wounds on his legs and abdomen, and blood soaked his uniform, but he was alive.

Nadia and I ran towards the man as the driver started the engine. Just as we were about to lift him into the ambulance, at that moment, the Israelis started to shoot at us. We threw the soldier and ourselves into the back of the ambulance and the driver accelerated away. As bullets sprayed the bodies nearby we flung ourselves over the wounded man. The ambulance raced from the square, its doors flapping wildly. Nadia and I hung on desperately. Then the ambulance swerved violently. Nadia lost her grip and slipped out of the back.

I shouted at the driver. 'Stop! Stop now! Nadia has fallen out! We must get her!'

Even though I was yelling at the top of my voice, the driver couldn't hear with so much shooting and chaos all around. The road was now jammed with civilian cars. Horns were tooting wildly. Fighting back tears and terror, I prayed for Nadia's protection. Was she hurt? What would happen to her? How could I find her in this crowd? Would she be able to find her way back to the hospital?

There was more pandemonium when we arrived at the hospital. All my nursing experience in the hospitals in Beirut had not prepared me for the devastation of this full-scale attack. Within less than an hour the corridors and rooms were filled with wounded civilians. People were screaming and crying. There were women, children and old people on the floors, with limbs shattered and blood pouring through gaping abdominal wounds. Relatives of the wounded held them, their clothes soaked in blood too, crying and begging for help. Nurses and doctors were rushing from one person to the next, slipping in the pools of blood on the floor, trying to treat as many as they could. It was a truly horrific sight. The hospital was only a very small civilian Lebanese hospital with few beds and fewer facilities.

All I could think was, 'My God, if all of these people are wounded in just one hour of bombing, what will happen next?'

Then the bombing started again, and more and more wounded civilians poured into the hospital. I left the wounded Palestinian officer in the emergency room to be attended to by the doctors. As I left him, telling him the doctors would treat his arm, he whispered, 'Please contact my family in Jordan. Tell them what has happened. Tell them I love them all.' I reassured him I would, adding that he would soon be able to talk to them himself.

I went to help the nurses who were giving whatever first aid they could to the endless stream of people who kept staggering in through the hospital doors. Completely overwhelmed, the two doctors were glad of all the help they could get. Then as if by a miracle, Nadia appeared. We fell into each other's arms and hugged, both crying with relief and grief. She told us that when she had fallen out a passing motorist had picked her up and brought her to the hospital. I felt as if God had answered my prayers.

The attack intensified. We all knew the Israeli forces would enter the town centre any time now. One of the Lebanese doctors advised us to leave immediately as he knew we were Palestinians and the hospital staff would not be able to protect or hide us. We all understood that we would be taken prisoner or even killed if we were found by the invading soldiers. Even the hospital was not safe. We later learned this clearly marked Lebanese civilian hospital, called

Al Iman Hospital, was also bombed that day by the Israelis. Even more people died.

Before leaving, I went to check on the wounded officer we had brought in from the square. I searched the hospital and finally found him on the floor of a room filled with a growing number of dead. Knowing his family would want him back with them in Jordan, we put his body in the ambulance along with that of the man we had collected from Damour. The Palestinian Red Crescent emblem on the ambulance would make us a target, however, so we covered it with mud. Then we set off again thinking we could travel over the mountains to the Beqaa Valley, knowing it was no longer possible to go to Beirut as Israeli forces now controlled the Beirut/Damascus highway. Many civilians desperately trying to flee the fighting were being killed on the road, with cars being hit by tank shells and strafed by planes. This meant we could not reach the Beqaa Valley via the main highway either.

Around 5 p.m. we found our way to one of the Lebanese Army military bases in the Aley area, telling the soldiers we were Palestinian medical workers and needed to leave the area immediately. They advised us to drive through the mountains to the Beqaa Valley via a longer, but safer military road, warning that if we strayed from the road, we would end up in an Israeli-controlled area.

Our anxiety ratcheted up, as none of us knew the area. Seeing this, they offered to send a fighter with us who knew the route well. With our welcome escort, we left, although by now it was dark but still very hot, and we were exhausted. The bodies of the two men, though wrapped and protected, were starting to decompose in the back of the ambulance, with the accompanying overpowering smell that was making us feel very nauseous. I prayed we would manage to get to the Palestinian hospital at Bar Elias in the Beqaa Valley unscathed. Although I was exhausted, the terror of being caught and taken prisoner kept me alert. My eyes stayed glued to the dark road ahead as my stomach churned, my throat tightened, and I fought to keep my fear from overwhelming me.

It was a long and tortuous route through the mountains. Thank God, it was summer: in winter it would have been covered with snow and we would never have been able to escape via that route.

With enormous relief we finally arrived in an area controlled by the Syrian army. This was where our guide had to leave us and return to his unit. He told us to just keep going—it was 2 a.m. on June 11 and just 36 hours after we'd left Beirut. We were safe. We had survived.

8

BACK TO BEIRUT

I was in the Beqaa Valley and was safe, but my joy was short-lived as the staff at the hospital updated us on the Israeli invasion, coordinated by Israeli Defence Minister, Ariel Sharon. Within hours of our escape from Damour, it had fallen. A vicious and sustained ground attack and aerial bombing campaign on Lebanon's southern cities of Sidon, Tyre and Nabatiyeh had left the cities in ruins, thousands of Lebanese civilians dead or wounded, and hundreds of thousands left homeless. Worse things happened in the nearby Palestinian refugee camps of Ain al-Helwah, al-Bas, Burj al-Shemali and Rachidiyeh. More than 10,000 Palestinians lost their lives and more than 6000 Palestinians and Lebanese were taken prisoner in this initial three-day assault in southern Lebanon. Many of the prisoners were severely beaten, some to death, and the survivors were denied food and water for days. All refugee camps in the south were severely damaged and Ain al-Helwah was destroyed, bombed and then bulldozed so that nothing remained. Hundreds of thousands of miserable Palestinian camp homes were flattened.

By the Friday, June 11, Beirut was under siege from the Israeli attackers. International concern at the overwhelming force of the Israeli occupation mounted and, diplomatic efforts were being focused on achieving a ceasefire between Israel and the PLO and leftist forces. The first of many of these was agreed on the next day, June 12, but the bombings, fighting and siege of Beirut continued. In Tel Aviv on June 26 the Israeli people vented their outrage with 10,000 protesters demanding an immediate withdrawal of the Israeli army from Lebanon.

On 3 July, under considerable Arab and international pressure, Arafat signed a pledge to withdraw PLO fighters from Beirut. Incomprehensibly, the next day on Sharon's orders all food, fuel, water and electricity supplies were cut to the city's 600,000 civilians. It took nearly six weeks until August 18 for the final details of the Israeli and PLO withdrawals to be finalised, including details on how, in the PLO's absence, US and UN forces would protect the Palestinian refugees. Throughout this time, the people of Beirut and the camps suffered extraordinary hardship and deprivation. For those Lebanese, I am sure they often looked to our camps as the source of their troubles rather than where it truly lay—at Sharon's feet.

After the invasion, Walid Jumblatt withdrew his Druze militia from the Lebanese National Movement, greatly diminishing its strength. Under pressure from the UN and US, a broadly representative Lebanese National Salvation Committee was formed, and on August 21, with Israeli tanks ringing the Lebanese Parliament buildings, Bashir Gemayel, head of the Christian Lebanese Forces and the only candidate standing, was elected President of Lebanon. The Israelis had refused to allow a UN protection force to be deployed. Instead a US-led Multinational Force (MNF) took up the role of protector as the PLO withdrew from Beirut on September 9. There was little protection for the Lebanese population in West Beirut and none, except the written word of the US and UN, for the 85,000 or so Palestinian refugees in Beirut or the other 350,000 or more in camps across Lebanon.

For the three months that terror rained down on my family and friends in Beirut, I remained trapped in the Beqaa Valley, deeply concerned for their safety. We were not permitted by the Lebanese government to have phones in the camp—they were considered a sign of permanent settlement—so I had no idea if my family was still there, given the camps were being targeted in the air strikes. Nor did my family know whether I was still alive. It took about 10 days to get a message to my parents via the Red Cross and I had scant news of them.

Eventually I received news that my family had fled to my uncle's flat just outside the camp when the invasion started, but that as the war escalated and the flat also became unsafe, they had relocated, along with thousands of others, to the city's business centre in the Hamra district. There they stayed for a night in one of the many disused hotels before my uncle was able to find them a flat. They were the lucky ones; many refugees had to make the bombed-out or empty hotels—tourists having fled Beirut during the war—their home. Many refugees from the south and the southern suburbs of Beirut also sought shelter in the hotels' underground carparks—each family occupying a couple of car spaces, with blankets hung to create the illusion of walls and privacy.

Desperate to be with my family, I kept myself busy as a way to stop worrying. There was plenty of work for us in the small PRCS hospital in Bar Elias, what with the fighting in the valley and air strikes on nearby towns such as Chtaura, where many civilians were wounded and killed. Working in the emergency room, I occasionally went with the ambulances to provide first aid to the wounded and bring them to the hospital, but unlike in Beirut, I felt safe, so in between emergencies, I had time for other activities.

Accommodation was, of course, difficult to find so I found myself sharing a room in the hospital with a woman named Fatima Bernawie. In the 1960s, Fatima had been fighting the Israelis in occupied Palestine, and became the first Palestinian woman to be taken prisoner. On her release, she had been exiled by the Israeli government to Jordan and had then travelled to Lebanon. One of her roles in the Beqaa was to make social and morale-boosting visits to the fighters in the bases. She would take newspapers and talk with the young men. She was full of energy and determination, which along with her strength and resilience, I really admired. She became a strong influence on me. From time to time Fatima would invite me to visit the fighter bases with her.

Of course, going to the military bases was dangerous—at any time we could have been killed. When on one occasion, Israeli planes started to bomb a base we were visiting, we hid with some of the fighters under trees a little distance from the base. As we lay on the ground, I remembered how the bombs from similar planes had destroyed huge buildings in Beirut and my mind filled with images of what could happen to us should a bomb hit where we lay. I saw us completely disappearing into the dust and my body in pieces. I looked around and saw boys lying flat in the fields nearby. There was dust and debris everywhere, but no one was hurt. We hid for more than 15 minutes, praying for protection as the bombing continued. When the attack was over I shared my thoughts with Fatima. She said, 'Yes, it is true the trees will not protect you, but you will not be seen easily. Also, my dear, remember that if something happens, it will happen. Neither the trees nor the buildings will protect you.'

Her words held true for me when on another day, without warning, Israeli planes bombed the centre of the little town of Chtaura. I was with a group that had gone for a day out. We had just bought ice-cream at one of the shops and were in the street when the bombing started, so we rushed for shelter. When the bombing was over we saw that the ice-cream shop had been hit, and everyone inside was killed. I remembered Fatima's words and accepted what fate would offer. My time was not yet up.

❖❖❖

They say that love is found in the strangest places. It is a truism for which I can vouch. Just as it seemed that the world around me was in flames, I met up again with my school friend, Mahmoud. He had received a PLO scholarship to Russia to study cinema photography and like many of the overseas students, had come back as a volunteer during the 1982 Israeli invasion, and was stationed in the Beqaa Valley. He, along with other young students who had lived in our camp, came and visited me in the hospital and all of us, as a large group, would sit together and talk.

I was 22 years old. Mahmoud and I had been friends for four years and had shared many experiences. He was tall, handsome and had a wicked sense of fun that shone out of his mischievous eyes; I loved the way that in spite of our terrible situation, he would always find something to joke about. I, on the other hand, was quiet and serious, but he could make me laugh—a trait that I never got sick of. Picking up where we had left off in our teenage years, we instantly reconnected, talking of our experiences in the war, and Mahmoud helping to calm me over my concerns for my family. Of course, we never met alone, but that did not stop the inevitable happening—we fell in love.

After several weeks, Mahmoud suggested we marry and I go back to Russia with him. I was very much in love but thought carefully about our situation. I wanted to marry him, yet at the same time I foresaw many difficulties with his proposal generally and was very torn. I wanted to return to my family in Beirut and continue my nursing. As well, I had been offered a scholarship to London from the UK Palestinian educational support group, UNIPAL. Even though I would be with Mahmoud, going to Russia would entail learning a new language and starting my career from scratch. I simply was just not yet ready to be away for many years from all the people I loved. We discussed all these things at length, so as a compromise he suggested we get engaged. But I did not want to be engaged either, as I knew we would be apart for a long time; and neither of us knew what the future held. I knew only that if we made a promise to each other and he broke it, I would never forgive him. We agreed to leave things as they were, to leave our fate to the future.

By early September the siege of the Lebanese capital had been lifted, our fighters had left Lebanon and the Israelis had withdrawn to the edge of the city. But the main Beirut/Damascus highway was still controlled by Israel and the Christian Lebanese Forces, so getting through was difficult. My desire to return to my family became overwhelming, but without an identity card I couldn't travel. During the war, with government not functioning, local *mukhtars*, village leaders, had been given the authority to issue identity papers. The grandfather of a Lebanese nursing friend was a *mukhtar*, so I asked him to help me with a new, but false, Lebanese identity card using my friend's details but with my photo. Because of my friendship with his granddaughter, he agreed. He trusted me to not use it for other things and to destroy the card once I got home to the camp.

I spent one night learning all about her cousins, her aunts and uncles and all her family, in case anyone at the Lebanese-controlled checkpoints knew her or members of her extended family. I then found a taxi driver willing to take me to Beirut. He told me it would be best to leave very early in the morning since there were fewer checkpoints then. My friends at the hospital suggested I should go to the hairdresser, have my hair done really nicely, put on lots of make-up and wear jeans and a blouse without sleeves. We all knew if I dressed in black or was covered in any way, as was generally expected of Muslim women, I was more likely to be stopped and questioned. I promised my friends I would contact them to let them know when I arrived safely. They'd become like family to me, so I found it hard to leave. Of course, they were also very anxious about the trip, but they also knew how long I'd wanted to return to my parents. Mahmoud was very much opposed to me leaving at that time because he felt that it was too dangerous. But I was determined; I knew he would try to stop me, so I left without saying goodbye.

With one of my friends, I caught a taxi first to Baalbek in order to catch my taxi to Beirut. Hurriedly saying goodbye, I hopped in the taxi hoping my make-up and sleeveless T-shirt, would camouflage me from harm. It was early in the morning and, though it was hot in the valley, up in the mountains the air was clear and cool. From the mountain roads the valley looked exquisitely beautiful. We passed with ease through the Syrian checkpoints to Bhamdoun and then, instead of continuing down the highway to Aley, where the roads remained closed to all civilian traffic, we turned right towards East Beirut.

Driving through the mountain suburbs of East Beirut, the taxi driver warned me when we neared a checkpoint. There were more than 15 in all. Fortunately, he was well known and chatted easily with the soldiers as we passed through the joint Israeli-Christian Lebanese Forces checkpoints. At each stop, I struggled to keep my hands from shaking, endeavouring to fix a smile on my face, terrified that any physical manifestation of my fear would reveal my deception—if I was caught, I would in all likelihood be raped, killed and 'disappeared', as so many others had been. Just passing Israeli tanks and the Lebanese militia scared me nearly to death. To calm myself throughout the journey, I recited an Islamic prayer of protection, asking God to place a block between myself and the dangers I might face. For one hour and 15 unrelenting minutes we wound our way back to Beirut—the longest 75 minutes I have yet to endure. But God was protecting me, and no one checked my papers. They just waved us through.

When we finally arrived in West Beirut and I realised I had survived and was now safe, I wanted to shout and jump with joy. But there was little time to indulge my relief. I tore up the identity card as promised, took out my mirror and removed all my make-up as a mark of respect for people who had lost relatives, then put my hair up, pulled on my long-sleeved shirt and set out to find my family.

During the siege, the PRCS had been forced to evacuate the camp hospitals of Gaza and Akka, moving everything to temporary hospitals in Hamra. One of them was in a church and I knew my younger sister, Mervat, was working there. In the city streets, everything was quiet; very few people were around. It was only now I could see the devastation the war had wrought. Many of the buildings had been badly damaged: some had their fronts sheared off, leaving the shattered insides exposed, as if in a macabre theatre set, most had been burnt out. All were pocked with bullet holes; no building was untouched. Whole buildings had collapsed. Huge slabs of concrete hung precariously and dangerously. Rubbish had not been collected. There was human waste everywhere. Burnt-out or bullet-riddled cars lay by the roadside. Here and there people had returned to live in these ruins and had put up blankets and makeshift covers to protect themselves from the elements. The few people I saw looked drained and haggard. Everything was black and sad.

Finally, I found where my sister was working. The minute we saw each other we burst into tears—we were so relieved to see each other alive. But I was desperate to see my parents. She told me that when I went missing, my father searched everywhere for information about me. He and all the family were sick with fear for my safety. Mervat said that he 'when no one could find you, he kept on saying that he felt as if all the sugar had left his body'. And indeed, my father's diabetes started at this time. Mervat told me when the fighting had stopped, and the Israelis had withdrawn to the edge of the city, people had returned to their homes in the camps. I left Mervat and made my way to Burj Barajneh, seeing the camp through the blur of my tears.

The destruction here was on a scale I could not have imagined. Many homes had been completely destroyed—bombed into oblivion. Those that were still standing were by any measure uninhabitable. There were huge gaping holes where rooms had once been. I could look into the middle of many houses because whole walls had been blown away. Pitiful attempts by returning residents at privacy and warmth failed as worn, bullet-riddled blankets flapped in the wind and people's pinched faces showed the strain of struggling to survive. There was evidence of tank fire, strafing and shooting everywhere. The water pipes had been ripped open, narrow lanes were soggy and slippery underfoot and electricity wires were cut and hanging dangerously low. Rubble made walking through the camp difficult. I held my breath as I neared my parents' house, not knowing what emotion to feel when I saw it still standing. It was badly damaged. The second floor, new and so proudly built, had bullet holes in the walls and doors. Yet there was my family—alive and safe. I was so overjoyed to see my parents, brothers and sisters, but inside, I was crying, for all my people and all the suffering they had endured.

◈◈◈

Despite the city and the camp being in ruins, life continued as it always does. I returned to work and buried myself in helping patients. It was the beginning of autumn when I returned to work at Akka Hospital. Rain was falling softly, and the day was warm and humid. The hospital, in a Lebanese area adjacent to the Sabra and Shatila refugee camps, was around 20 minutes walk from Burj Barajneh, along the airport road, under Ghobeiry Bridge and then left towards the Kuwait Embassy. It was a small hospital with a general medical ward, a paediatric ward and a rehabilitation centre for disabled people where an Australian woman, Jean Calder, worked. As I approached the hospital I could see it was extensively damaged. Even though the building had been clearly marked with large red crosses and red crescents, the Israelis had still bombed it.

The nursing school and all the administration buildings had been ransacked, as had the operating theatres, nursery and rehabilitation centre. Because of the damage, we had only a few patients and minimal equipment to deal with them. The hospital kitchen had also been destroyed, forcing us to buy food for the patients. There were six Palestinian nurses and three doctors in the hospital, as well as a laboratory technician, a pharmacist and cleaners, guards and cooks, (mostly Egyptian) and some administration staff. Several foreigners, mostly European nurses, were living there too.

◈◈◈

After the PLO and Syrian army left Beirut, the Israeli army stayed near the airport, leaving the city in the control of the Lebanese army. Camp residents were busy trying to repair their houses. When the UN Multinational Force withdrew on 10 September, 12 days before its scheduled departure, the Lebanese army moved into West Beirut.

The Palestinians, aware the right-wing Christian Lebanese Forces had been incorporated into the Lebanese army and that there were no armed PLO soldiers in the camps to protect them, became extremely anxious. In the agreement under which the PLO left Lebanon, Palestinians in the camps had been assured of protection by the US and the UN. But we all wondered if their assurances would be enough.

9

THE MASSACRE

On the evening of Monday, 13 September 1982, I went with two other nurses to buy food for patients. When we reached a Lebanese army checkpoint on the road from the hospital to the Ghobeiry area, soldiers stopped us and an officer asked us where we were going.

'To the bakery and the restaurant,' I replied.

'Why are you walking alone?'

'You know we can walk alone. Should we be afraid? What's wrong? Is there a problem?'

To our amazement, the officer said, 'Aren't you afraid of the Palestinians in the camp?'

'Why should I be afraid of my own people?' I asked, astonished.

The officer looked surprised. He would not believe we were Palestinians until we showed him our refugee papers.

'I imagined Palestinians differently,' he said.

The following night, we were cleaning and tidying up in the emergency area when one of the doctors walked in grim-faced to tell us Bashir Gemayel—just days before his inauguration as president—had been killed in a bomb blast.

The next morning, I again walked out to buy food, and came across the army officer from the previous day at the checkpoint.

'Are you happy now?' he asked.

'What's the matter with you?' I exclaimed. 'One day you ask me if I am afraid, and the next you ask me if I am happy. Why are you asking me these questions?'

'Don't tell me Bashir Gemayel's death means nothing to you,' he said.

I remained studiously polite. 'I have respect for the dead and I pray for them,' I said.

His tone changed. 'You Palestinians are the cause of everything bad that happens in Lebanon.'

I'd become used to this kind of accusation from certain Lebanese people. Even so, the way he spat the words out angered and distressed me.

'No, it's not because of us,' I said. 'You should read your history. There were many problems in Lebanon long before we were forced to flee Palestine in 1948. The problems in Lebanon are between the Maronites, the Christians and the Muslims, not between the Lebanese and the Palestinians.'

He became furious then. 'Do you know what I want to do?' he shouted. 'I want to go into that camp there and kill you. I want to kill all Palestinians.'

It finally dawned on me at this point that he believed Palestinians had killed Gemayel, although the Christian Lebanese man responsible by then had been arrested.[17] I knew if he thought that, plenty of others in the army would, too, as its ranks had been swollen by members of Gemayel's Christian Lebanese Forces militia. His anger made my anxious—I knew we were vulnerable in the refugee camps. We had no protection there at all.

---

17 Habib Shartouni, a member of the Syrian Social Nationalist Party, was sentenced to death in absentia in October 2017 by the Lebanese Justice Council. The Lebanese authorities arrested Shartouni after the assassination in 1982, but he was not prosecuted. In 1990, when the Syrian Army seized the Lebanese presidential palace Shartouni was smuggled from prison to an unknown location—Reuters World Service, October 21, 2017. 2.20 a.m.
https://www.reuters.com/article/us-lebanon-politics-trial/lebanese-court-issues-death-sentence-over-1982-gemayel-assassination

Two hours after this exchange, the soldiers left the checkpoint. We were so happy to see them go. But within minutes of their departure, Israeli tanks and soldiers took over the position. Had there'd been an arrangement between the two armies? Then heard on the radio that Israel's Defence Minister Ariel Sharon, and his chief of staff, Lieutenant-General Rafael Eitan, had broken the US-sponsored ceasefire agreement, ordering Israeli troops from their positions south of the airport back into Beirut's southern suburbs. We could see them stationed all around Akka Hospital and knew they must have surrounded the nearby refugee camp of Shatila as well. While we weren't sure what all this meant, we did know that during their occupation of south Lebanon, the Israelis had arrested male doctors and nurses as well as male patients. This gave us cause to be seriously worried for all the males in Akka Hospital; it was possible the Israelis might take the rest of us prisoner too.

Hiam, a Lebanese Druze nurse, and I decided to volunteer to see what would happen if we tried to leave the hospital in our uniforms. We knew if *we* could get out, it might be possible for the young male doctors and staff to leave too, as we feared what might happen to them if they stayed and were caught. The moment we stepped out of the hospital, Israeli soldiers stationed around it rudely ordered us back inside. Hiam and I told them we were nurses on duty. One of the soldiers said, 'No, go back inside! They won't hurt you. Go back!'

I was confused. What did the soldier mean by saying 'they' wouldn't hurt us? Who were 'they'?

I had a premonition that something terrible was about to happen, but when we contacted Umm Walid, the head of the PRCS (Palestinian Red Crescent Society) in Beirut, on our walkie-talkie, she tried to reassure us. The PLO had left and there were no fighters or weapons in the camps, only unarmed civilians, so there was no pretext for an attack on the camps. Umm Walid said she believed the military redeployment was due to Gemayel's assassination and she suggested we stay put. Camp residents didn't share her confidence, however, fearing a resurgence of fighting. Hundreds of people from

Shatila, mostly women, young children and the elderly, crowded into the shelter under the hospital. The men and older children stayed behind in the camp to look after their homes. As well as Jean Calder, the Australian physiotherapist, we had nurses from Norway, Denmark and Sweden working at the hospital. We also had a French journalist with us at the time. We desperately hoped the presence of foreigners would give us some protection.

Not long after the Israeli troops took up their positions, we heard Israeli planes flying over the camps, followed by shelling and small-arms fire. Fighters from the Lebanese resistance movements had started attacking the Israelis in the streets. There was no fighting in Shatila itself, but we could hear it in the streets around us. We were effectively trapped in the hospital. The fighting went on for hours and quite quickly we ran short of food and water for the patients, and we had no electricity or running water. One of the hospital administrators, Mr Orabie, had been shot and killed by the Israelis earlier in the day while he was trying to repair the hospital's water pipes. I was working in the emergency department at this stage and, because we had only a few patients, I offered to accompany two ambulance men who were about to drive to Gaza Hospital to fetch some food and water. The hospital lay on the other side of Shatila, less than five minutes away, in a poor Lebanese area called Sabra. In the poorer districts, outsiders often had difficulty differentiating between Lebanese and Palestinian enclaves, so the two were lumped together as Sabra Shatila.

We loaded a young man into the ambulance who was too badly wounded for us to treat, and the French journalist joined us as well. In hindsight, it seems a crazy, foolhardy mission. But we had no way of knowing how long the lockdown would last, and we could not stand by and see our patients die with lack of food and especially without water for drinking as well as washing. The moment we drove out of the hospital and began to cross the road into Shatila, the Israelis, positioned just up the road near the Kuwaiti Embassy, fired a heavy volley at us, even though our ambulance was clearly marked.

The driver yelled to us to get down. He was driving without looking, his head below the level of the dashboard.

Once inside the camp, we were safe for the time being. We drove down the small roads to Gaza Hospital, where everything was quiet, and saw no fighters, militia or soldiers in the camp. It was late afternoon and the shooting around the camp had waned. Our colleagues at Gaza Hospital gave us food, hummus, bread and water. We drove back through the small camp lanes to a point just across the road from our (Akka) hospital. There we stopped, knowing that if we tried to drive across the road we'd be shot at. In the end we got out of the ambulance and, when the coast seemed clear, sprinted over to the hospital entrance carrying only a small quantity of the much-needed provisions. Later, when the fighting had died down completely, one of our drivers, Nabil Maroof, was able to bring the ambulance, with the rest of the food and water, into the hospital grounds.

On the afternoon of Thursday 16 September, representatives of the people in the shelter and camp, decided to approach the Israelis to reassure them there were no fighters in the camp. They split into two groups of about 50, each carrying white flags. One grup turned left outside the hospital gates and headed up the hill towards the Israeli position near the Kuwaiti Embassy, and the other turned right and walked down the road to the bridge. After a short while the group that had gone towards the embassy returned, asking about the people who had gone towards the bridge. We told them they had not returned. The people in the embassy group became worried. We'd been under the impression that Lebanese army soldiers were there. But the embassy group had learned the bridge checkpoint was manned by Israeli soldiers and militiamen from Gemayel's Christian Lebanese Forces. The Palestinian civilians, elderly men and women, who'd gone to the bridge checkpoint carrying white flags and seeking peace never came back. They disappeared. We later learned they'd all been executed.

That night the camp was illuminated by 'light bombs'—flares. We couldn't work out what was happening. All we knew was the Israeli army had surrounded the camp and there were probably Christian Lebanese Forces among them. Since the Lebanese leftist groups still in West Beirut could not enter the camp and all PLO fighters had left, there couldn't possibly be any fighting inside. So why were the Israelis firing flares? Throughout Friday, we could hear shelling and small-arms fire as the Israelis clashed with Lebanese leftists, apparently in a street nearby.

We remained trapped inside the hospital, still with no electricity and once again short of food, water and medicines for the patients. The street fighting decreased during the afternoon and by the early evening everything was quiet. Seeing that some in the hospital craved coffee and cigarettes, I and another nurse slipped across the road to a small shop in the camp. While we were there, two young boys in a state of near-hysteria came in yelling that someone was in the camp killing people. We didn't believe them but suggested they come back with us to the hospital anyway. At the hospital we told the doctors the boys' story, but no one thought it was true.

With little left to eat and no place to prepare meals for the people in the hospital shelter, several women set off to their homes to fetch food for their children. Soon after they'd gone, one returned, screaming there'd been a massacre in the camp and her family had been slaughtered. Her husband and other children had been stabbed and their throats slit, she said. Her clothes were covered in blood where she'd been holding her dead husband. She was hysterical. We all asked ourselves how murderers could enter the camp and do such things with the Israeli army surrounding it. We knew the Israelis would fight us, but we couldn't believe they would massacre us. We thought the killing must be the act of some deranged individual acting alone, and we tried to calm her.

At one point, our two ambulance drivers set off for Gaza Hospital to pick up drugs we needed urgently. Their vehicle was clearly marked as an ambulance. Instead of going through Shatila, they tried to take a longer route around it. They never returned. We later learned they were stopped, hauled out of the ambulance and executed by soldiers in an area where both the Lebanese Forces and Israelis were stationed.

That flares again lit up the camp area, turning night into day. Why were the Israelis doing this? To make ourselves laugh, we joked that they knew we had no electricity and wanted to give us some light. Food and water ran out completely during the night. We received only one casualty but knew from our radio exchanges with Gaza Hospital that it had received many on Wednesday night and on Thursday, though we had no details. We thought they were from the fighting in the surrounding streets. We found our lone casualty after hearing a weak cry for help in a street near the hospital. On investigating, we found a boy of about 13 with a bullet wound in his chest. His name was Mofid Muhammad. We took him immediately to the operating theatre where, without anaesthetic, water and electricity, Dr Mohammad al Khatib inserted a chest tube. He said that in the morning we should try to take the boy to Gaza Hospital, which had better facilities.

When I talked to the boy, he said, 'They came... They killed my father, they killed my brother, they tried to kill me. I pretended I was dead. When they left the house, I crawled away to the hospital.'

I asked him who had done these things.

'They were speaking with a funny Arabic accent. They came into the house swearing and shooting, saying they would kill all Palestinians.'

I went and reported to Dr Mohammad what the boy had said. By now it was becoming clear to us people were indeed being butchered in the camp. A sickening fear began to weigh heavily in the pit of my stomach. Dr Mohammad and I looked at each other.

'What do I say?' he asked, despairingly. 'Do I tell everyone there's a massacre taking place in the camp? There are hundreds of people in the bomb shelter under the hospital. What will happen if we tell them? Where can they go? We're surrounded and trapped here. The Israelis have already shot at us when we've tried to move. We have to stay quiet and calm and pray no one will enter the hospital. Let's try to contact Gaza Hospital on the walkie-talkie and find out what's happening there now.'

Dr Mohammad, myself, and a nurse named Iman Massar went to the men who had the walkie-talkie and asked them to contact Gaza Hospital. As Dr Mohammad was speaking over the radio to the hospital, men with heavy Lebanese accents intercepted the call and began to abuse us. Using foul street language, they told us that they would break into the hospital at midnight and rape the women and kill the men. I was sickened at the way they talked to us. Their ugly threats made us feel more frightened and powerless than ever. There was really nothing we could do. Undoubtedly those men would kill us if we tried to leave the hospital. I was gripped by a kind of fear I'd never known before. I told Iman I didn't want anyone to touch me; that to be raped without trying to resist would be unthinkable. I said that when those men entered the hospital they would probably shoot wildly, and I would prefer to die by the bullet than be caught and raped.

We told no one about the walkie-talkie conversation; the last thing we wanted to do was terrify the other nurses and hospital workers. Iman and I were working in the emergency department so since we had no patients at that time, we decided to sit by the main gate hoping when the attack came we'd be shot first. We sat there from 11.30 p.m. for about four and a half hours. It felt like 100 years. I couldn't think of anything other than saying goodbye to the world, to life. Now and then we'd try to make ourselves laugh. We'd say silly things and laugh hysterically. But all the time I felt death was a moment away. I felt as if we were in another world.

By 4 o'clock in the morning of Saturday 18 September, we were ready to collapse. We decided to go inside and get some sleep. Opposite the emergency room was a small clinic. There we took off our shoes and lay on the floor—without mattresses or covers—and slept until 7 o'clock. On waking, I was actually amazed to find we were still alive, and immediately wondered if everyone else had survived. I carefully opened the door and saw our three doctors (Mohammad al Khatib, Sami al Khatib and Ali Othman) and nurses working in the emergency room. Nothing had happened. The murderers hadn't come. The Israelis still surrounded the hospital and the camp. Those men on the radio must have just been trying to terrorise us.

Not long after we woke, however, we heard shooting and screams. Our relief at finding ourselves alive quickly dissipated, the gnawing fear returning. The terrifying sounds went on for about 10 minutes, to be replaced by an eerie silence. During this interlude an old man, Abu Ali, a PRCS bus driver whose house in Shatila stood directly opposite the hospital, decided to risk the dash across the road to get food for the staff. He made it safely, but just as he was about to open his front door, he heard voices in a neighbouring house. It sounded as though men were consulting a map and discussing how to attack the hospital. The old man ran back to warn us. All of us in the emergency department looked at each other in silence. At that moment, with hundreds of people in the shelter, we knew the huge responsibility we faced.

Around 10 o'clock, a Lebanese woman came running into the hospital from a poor Lebanese area called Hursh which was near Sabra. Militiamen had entered this area and accidentally slaughtered many Lebanese, thinking they were Palestinians. When they discovered their error, they stopped the massacre and let remaining residents out through the ring of Israeli soldiers around the camp. This Lebanese woman knew us well, however, as she had often brought her children to us for treatment over the years.

'The murderers told me they were planning to kill everyone in the hospital,' she cried. 'Please, you must leave now!'

'We can't. It's impossible. We've already tried—without success. The Israeli army is all around us,' I said—I prayed she'd heard incorrectly.

In the midst of a desperate discussion about what we should do to save our patients and the people in the shelter, we noticed the Israelis had suddenly withdrawn from the checkpoint under the bridge. A gap had unexpectedly opened up in the armed ring around the camp. Several of us hurried down to the people in the shelter and told them to get out of the hospital immediately. We told them that once outside, they should turn right and run under the Ghobeiry bridge towards the Haret Hreik and the Shiyah areas, to get as far away from Shatila as possible.

Now we faced a dilemma. How could we get all of the non-ambulant patients out of the hospital? After telling those who could walk to leave immediately, we began discussing what to do with the bedridden patients. The foreign nurses urged us to go quickly, saying they would look after the remaining patients. As foreigners, they were bound to be safe, they insisted.

Dr Mohammad was reluctant to go. 'It's our duty to stay,' he insisted. 'And as doctors and nurses, we'll be safe.'

'As safe as all those nurses and doctors slaughtered in Tel al-Za'atar?' I reminded them.

The tense discussion went back and forth, with the foreign nurses urging us to leave immediately. Suddenly we were interrupted by the sound of intense gunfire at the hospital entrance. The Lebanese militia were attacking from the position the Israelis had just vacated. Dr Ali, Dr Mohammad, Iman, several other nurses and I were on the ground floor. We ran to a window at the back of the hospital, clambered out and ran into the garden of a villa owned by an Armenian family behind the hospital. Dr Ali, who had a paralysed leg, was doing his best to keep up with us. The front gate of the villa was locked; the only way out was over the fence. Several of us tried to help Dr Ali scale the fence but he found it impossible. He and two of the nurses opted to hide inside the villa. Once over the fence, we ran for our lives towards the bridge and then scattered. As I ran, I thought that what was happening in Shatila might also be happening in Burj Barajneh, so instead of heading home, I made for Haret Hreik, a suburb sandwiched between the two camps. Haifa Hospital in Burj camp had been damaged beyond use during the Israeli invasion, and I knew its staff were in a makeshift but empty hospital in Haret Hreik. I knew my sister, Mervat, was there too.

She was asleep when I found her.

'Don't you know what's happening?' I was crying, out of breath, in total shock. 'The Lebanese and Israelis are massacring our people!'

However, neither she nor the others there believed me. The doctors thought the presence of the Israeli army had made me hysterical; they wanted to give me an injection of Valium to settle me. I left and ran to my uncle's place. I thought that, as a journalist, he might know what was happening. He rang the newspaper he worked for but none of the other journalists had heard anything. While I was there, my mother happened to come by.

'My dear, why are you making up these terrible rumours and frightening us?' she scolded.

'Why won't people believe me?' I cried. 'I am not imagining this! People have been slaughtered. The militiamen are in the hospital and are killing nurses and doctors. You've got to believe me!' At that point, I turned around and walked out.

In a daze I headed back towards the Ghobeiry bridge where the Lebanese army was now stationed. An officer stopped me, saying I couldn't go any further because there'd been a massacre. So, I returned to the makeshift hospital in Haret Hreik. By then the other nurses and Dr Mohammad had arrived and were quick to verify my story. Everyone stood frozen in silence. They knew the same thing could happen in this hospital. We were acutely conscious of our utter defencelessness, having no idea what to do, or where we could go. Later, I learned that when residents of Burj Barajneh—which apparently hadn't been surrounded—heard about the massacre, most fled. Hundreds ran wherever they could, terrified their camp would be next.

Not long afterwards, Israeli tanks rumbled down the street, loudspeakers blaring: 'We are the Israeli army. We are stronger than you. If you resist we will kill you.'

I stood watching them go by, convinced I was in a long and hideous nightmare from which, at any moment, I would wake to find none of this was happening. The Israelis drove arrogantly in their tanks through the streets of Haret Hreik and Burj Barajneh for several hours, harassing anyone they could find, before finally driving off to the airport.

Later that day we discovered what had happened to Dr Ali, Dr Sami and the other nurses and patients at Akka Hospital. The two nurses hiding in the villa with Dr Ali were Fariel Khalil—who was Palestinian but who grew up in a Lebanese village and therefore spoke with a Lebanese accent—and Antisar. Fariel's accent saved her, but the Lebanese Forces' militiamen could tell Antisar was Palestinian. They dragged her out of the villa and raped her. Then, as she lay screaming to be killed, they shot her. They tied Dr Sami, who'd remained inside the hospital building, and Dr Ali to jeeps, dragged them along the road in front of the hospital and finally shot them too. We heard from the foreign nurses at the hospital that militiamen went through the wards and found the young boy we'd treated for his chest wound. They pulled out his chest tube, threw him to the floor and kicked him like a football along the corridor, shouting repeatedly that all Palestinians should die. They kicked him to death.

The disabled children whom Jean Calder was looking after described the horror they'd been through. They said a militiaman stood at each end of the corridor and pushed the wheelchair-bound children back and forth along it, saying to them, 'You think we're going to kill you, don't you? No, no, we don't want to kill you. You're no threat to us. If all Palestinians were like you, it would be fine. You're disabled; you're nothing.'

In spite of pleas from the foreign nurses, many babies were killed, as were bedridden patients. Neither were hospital cooks, cleaners and guards—mostly Egyptian—spared, and the hospital was looted and burned. All the while, the Israeli army stood by and did nothing.

We heard that Lebanese militiamen had also killed nurses at Gaza Hospital. The foreign nurses and doctors working there testified that on the Saturday morning, as militiamen were marching them down the camp's main street, they saw hundreds of mainly women and children under guard sitting by a large and recently dug pit. Soon after this, they heard repeated shooting for 10 minutes or more, accompanied by screams and cries.

For two nights and days, the slaughter in Sabra and Shatila[18] took place without anyone outside the immediate area knowing about it, so tight was the clamp-down by the Israelis. Even in suburbs right next door, people were going about their daily business, buying and selling produce in the market, unaware of the slaughter happening at their doorstep.

For two days and nights after the massacre, I slept as if in a coma. I had nightmares filled with the people who'd been slaughtered; all the people I'd known and loved and who were no longer there. When I finally woke up, a black cloud of grief and despair had settled around me, shot through with flashes of terror that at any moment soldiers would come crashing through the door to kill me and my family. I couldn't bear to listen to the news, and I would burst into tears without apparent reason. I just wanted to run way from everything, but my limbs felt too heavy to move. My whole body felt leaden. And my throat was constricted constantly. Nothing seemed to shift it.

It took around six months for the black cloud to lift. But as my grief waned, it was replaced by a burning rage at what had happened. Even now, if I talk about these events, my fear and rage return and I know the nightmares will soon follow.

❖❖❖

No one knows exactly how many people died in Sabra and Shatila, but estimates run to about 2000, mostly old men, women and children, all unarmed and defenceless. Robert Fisk, the respected British journalist covering the Middle East at the time, described his entry into the camp around 10 a.m. on Saturday 18 September, which largely confirmed what we had heard.

---

18 Friedman, Thomas; 'The Beirut Massacre: The Four Days,' *New York Times*. http://www.nytimes.com/1982/09/26/world/the-beirut-massacre-the-four-days.html

They were everywhere, in the road, in the lane-ways, in backyards and broken rooms, beneath crumpled masonry and across the top of garbage tips. The murderers—the Christian militiamen whom Israel had let into the camps—had only just left. In some cases, the blood was still wet on the ground. When we had seen a hundred bodies we stopped counting. Down every alleyway, there were corpses—women, young men, babies and grandparents—lying together in terrible profusion where they had been knifed or machine-gunned to death. Each corridor through the rubble produced more bodies. Perhaps a thousand people were butchered; probably half that number again. Even while we were there, we could see the Israelis watching us. From the top of the tower block to the west—the second building on the Avenue Camille Chamoun—we could see them staring at us through field glasses, scanning back and forth across the streets of corpses. This was a mass killing ... It was a war crime.[19]

In the wake of global condemnation, the Israeli Government immediately set up a commission of inquiry into the massacre. Four months later, the Kahan Commission Report[20] was made public and confirmed what we knew—that Christian Lebanese Forces militiamen, with the Israeli army's connivance, had systematically tortured, raped and slaughtered innocent refugee women, children and old men between 6 p.m. on 16 September and the morning of 18 September. The report detailed how corpses were buried in mass graves dug by Israeli bulldozers. Those same bulldozers flattened houses, burying any further evidence.

The inquiry found Israeli officials, especially Defence Minister Ariel Sharon, and his Chief of Staff Lieutenant General Rafael Eitan, were independently responsible for the massacre because they should have known what would occur. It found Kata'eb leaders, the dominant Christian militia in the Lebanese Forces, had repeatedly made clear what they intended to do with Palestinians they found, and

19 Fisk, R. 1991, *Pity the Nation*, Touchstone, New York, p. 360.
20 Eban, A. 1983, *The Beirut Massacre: The Complete Kahan Commission Report*, Karz-Cohl, New York, p. 104.

some Israeli leaders had said candidly they hoped to 'purify' Lebanon of Palestinians. In its chilling account of the events, the commission's report left no doubt that Sharon and the most senior Israeli military personnel to the Lebanese Forces were partners in this war crime.

In one instance, the report says, Israeli officers sharing a command post with Lebanese Forces reported a conversation on the evening of September 16, in which a Lebanese officer inside the camp said he was holding more than 45 women, children and old men. When he asked his senior Lebanese officer what he should do with them, the reply was, 'Do the will of God'. By 8 o'clock, only two hours after the militiamen had entered the camp, according to the Kahan Commission Report, more than 300 people had already been killed—all civilians. The Israeli officers, having been in the command post with the militia leaders, were fully aware of these facts.

The commission's report also described how an Israeli battalion commander on the Friday night, realising Palestinians were being massacred, told his men, 'We know. It's not to our liking, but don't interfere.' In its recommendations, the commission found Sharon 'bears personal responsibility' for the massacre and recommended Israel's Prime Minister of the day remove him from office.[21] Sharon and several high-ranking military officials resigned, but Sharon's disgrace was short-lived—by 2001 all was forgotten, and he was elected Prime Minister of Israel. He never faced trial in a national or international war crimes' court for his part in this massacre. In fact, no one has ever faced trial. Like so many times in our history before, the world professed its shock at what had been done to Palestinian refugees—and then did nothing.

---

21 Eban, A. 1983, *The Beirut Massacre: The Complete Kahan Commission Report*, Karz-Cohl, New York, p. 104.

10

NAWAL'S BROTHER

A s we are always forced to do, I pushed my grief aside and went back to work straight away. Akka Hospital was in ruins, and there were no longer any patients there. So, I transferred to Gaza Hospital, taking on the role of night supervisor. To get to work, I had to walk through Sabra and Shatila camps, past the alleyways and homes that had witnessed such sadness, misery and horror just days before. Yet it seemed already the outside world had moved on.

On September 22, 1982, only four days after the Sabra and Shatila massacre, their work done and now under pressure from the US, the Israeli army withdrew to the airport perimeter. The next day, just seven days after Bashir Gemayel had been assassinated, his brother Amin was elected President. On September 29, 19 days after it had left the Palestinians unprotected, the US-led Multinational Force returned to Beirut.

The Israelis remained in East Beirut and in the mountains with their allies, the Lebanese Forces, and occupied all of south Lebanon. The Syrians were in the Beqaa Valley. There were no armed Palestinians in Beirut; and the Lebanese army, now with many Christian Lebanese Forces militia in its ranks, had control of West Beirut.

During this period there were mass arrests and detentions as the army set up checkpoints, searched homes and sent thousands of Palestinian and Lebanese radicals for interrogation in East Beirut. Leftist and communist party offices were raided and censorship regulations banning criticism of the army and government were reinstated. Shanty towns on the edge of Shatila and in the West Beirut beachfront area of Ouzie, were ruthlessly dismantled, once again displacing Shi'a Lebanese. By December 1982, more than 2000 people had been registered as missing, and of these, only 600 were Palestinian; the rest were Lebanese. The excesses of the army were greatly resented, so inevitably opposition movements grew. But with the PLO gone, the unprotected Palestinian refugees were an easy target; and life became a matter of survival.

One day I was walking through the camp on my way to Gaza Hospital when I saw a young Lebanese army officer, in a gesture of affection, put his hand on a small boy's head. Immediately, the boy started screaming and ran to the Italian peacekeepers, asking them to save him. I was really frightened that something had happened to the boy and walked over to investigate. The Lebanese officer turned to me and said, 'Please tell him that I don't want to hit him, I just want to play with him'. With tears running down his face, the soldier told me how sad he was that this small child had run away in fear. I remember that day well; it reminded me that all good people suffered in Lebanon.

That same night, a number of armed soldiers in Lebanese army uniform brought a wounded man into the hospital emergency room where I was working. Two Lebanese soldiers were on guard outside the hospital. Although there were UN peacekeepers in the camp, and they would visit the hospital occasionally, we had lost confidence in their ability to protect us. We felt they would not be able to stop the Christian Lebanese Forces if they wanted to massacre us again. The man these soldiers brought in was big. He'd been hit by bullets and was in a critical condition. We started to treat him immediately and called for the surgeon, Dr Fayez. While I worked, I noticed the armed soldiers were still in the emergency room. As arms were forbidden in the hospital, I politely asked them to leave.

In reply, one pointed his gun at me.

'If you don't shut your mouth, I'll close it for you,' he snapped roughly.

Under Dr Fayez's orders, we prepared to take the wounded man downstairs to the X-ray Department—as there was no electricity for the lifts to operate—but even with the help of the X-ray technician, he was too heavy for us. When I asked two of the soldiers if they would carry him, one of them replied, 'What, stupid woman! Do you want us to help you carry this (a string of oaths) *kelp* (dog) Palestinian.'

That's when I realised the patient was Palestinian. So now I wondered if these soldiers were regular Lebanese army officers or Lebanese Forces militiamen, many of whom were now in the army.

Struggling under the weight of the patient, we arrived at the X-ray Department, followed by the two soldiers. We placed the man on the X-ray table and the technician prepared the patient for his investigations. The technician and I then went behind the protection screen while the X-ray was taken. When he finished, I went to prepare the patient for return to the emergency department. At this point, one of the soldiers blocked my way while the other roughly pulled the patient's infusion line out and grabbed his head. Then, to my horror, he started to smash the patient's head viciously on the steel table. I yelled at him to stop and somehow pushed past his companion, grabbing his arm in an effort to stop him. The other soldier started hitting me in my back with his gun, shouting and swearing at me.

'Go away! Do you want to save his life? You should all be dead!'

He let the wounded man's head fall on the hard table. Blood was pouring from the patient's head and dripping on to the floor. With a last, desperate, gasp for air the man died. I stood staring at him. The X-ray technician was also rooted to the spot, staring. I did not believe what I'd seen. Yet all my instincts warned me the soldiers would likely turn on both of us, next.

Finding my courage—from where, I don't know—I turned to leave the room to fetch sheets to cover this poor man. The soldier who had been hitting me shouted, 'Where do you think you're going?'

As calmly as I could, I said, 'To get sheets to cover him. That is our culture.'

I went upstairs, the soldier following me, and found Dr Fayez in the emergency room. When he saw me, he knew immediately that something was seriously wrong.

'Olfat, what's the matter, you are so pale. What has happened?' I burst into tears.

'They killed him! They smashed his head on the X-ray table and they killed him!'

I was shaking with fear, while Dr Fayez had gone pale; I could see his hands were shaking too. I remembered the patients and nurses and doctors who had been murdered at Akka Hospital just a few weeks earlier. Would this murder signal more such barbarous acts were to follow? Frozen inside and not really thinking, I took the sheets.

Then the soldier, who had not left my side, said to Dr Fayez, 'Shall I tell you how we killed him? Do you want me to tell you how I killed him?' And he put his gun in my face. I was crying, terrified and horrified. Beyond thinking, now. Then he asked me, very roughly, 'Are you sure he is dead?'

'Yes, I am sure he is dead.'

After that, at gunpoint, Dr Fayez and I were marched downstairs to certify the man was dead. Together with another nurse, we wrapped the dead man in the sheet and took him to the morgue, followed by the soldiers who did not let us out of their sight. When we returned to the emergency room, they were joking, looking at us and making fun of our accents, using very rude and crude language.

Unable to help myself, I looked at them and said, 'If you wanted to kill this man, why did you bring him to the hospital, for God's sake?'

But then it occurred to me: they must have shot him inside the camp, and if the Italian peacekeepers had found the body these men would have been in trouble. They could kill with impunity in the hospital—after all, there were only Palestinians in the hospital and they would not dare to report them to the local authorities and would not be believed if they did. Any moment, though, I thought they would kill us, too, just to ensure there were no witnesses.

When I could, I unobtrusively asked one of the nurses to round up all the young male patients who could walk and take them to the fifth floor of the hospital—at that time, a storage area. I told her to get them to hide behind the stored beds and tables. After that, we had to tell the other staff what was happening. Like us, they were terrified that they, too, might be slaughtered. We could only pray for the patients we couldn't move to safety.

The two soldiers stayed in the hospital, taunting and threatening all the staff until 4 a.m. But before they left, one went to get something from their jeep, cutting his hand in the process. It was only a small cut, but he demanded that we put a dressing on it. We had no choice, being threatened at gunpoint. One of the other nurses and I went to the emergency room to get the necessary materials ready. When the soldier sat down, I noticed his army identity card in his back pocket. I desperately wanted to know his name so I could report him. While the other nurse was fitting his dressing, I stood behind him and gently eased his identity card from his pocket. After reading his details, I slipped the card on to the seat so that when he stood up he would think it had simply fallen out of his pocket.

The next morning one of the hospital cleaners, Nawal, who lived in the camp, arrived for work. She noticed we were all tired but rather than tell her what happened I responded in kind, 'You too look very tired, Nawal'. She told me she had not slept because the Lebanese militia had been chasing her brother through the camp and she did not know what had happened to him. It struck me then that the man who had been killed was probably her brother. I was able to call the hospital administrator who, without telling her about her brother's death suggested she go home and rest. Soon after, her relatives broke the news to her. I found it difficult to work that day. I cried for Nawal and her brother and I was deeply depressed and fearful at our weakened and vulnerable situation.

After I had given my verbal report on this murder to the Lebanese director of the hospital, he asked me to make a written report. This report was sent to the PRCS headquarters and I learned later it had been sent to the PLO leaders, who in turn sent it to the Lebanese government. Then without warning about 10 days later, as I did not know then what had happened to the report, two Lebanese army officers came to the hospital to interrogate me and the other nurse who had been on duty with me that night.

They returned again the next day and ordered us to go with them to East Beirut, where the government prison was and where many Palestinians, even women, had been taken. Many of our people had disappeared when they had gone there so we were fearful that would happen to us, too. As they did not have a written warrant, we refused to go with them. Instead we went to the Italian peacekeepers in the camp and told them we had been summoned for interrogation by the Lebanese army over this matter. They took our names and our parents' names and addresses, promising to check the hospital the following afternoon to make sure we had returned.

The next morning we went for interrogation with one of the Lebanese army soldiers guarding the hospital. I told these soldiers as well as the officers in the prison that I had informed the Italian peacekeepers where we were. At the security headquarters we were interviewed separately, but as I had written the report, my colleague was only briefly interrogated and then released. I was taken to a room and kept waiting for about four hours without food and drink.

Later that day three senior Lebanese army officers interrogated me. They began by shouting, 'You are a Palestinian woman! Where did you get the courage to write this report against the Lebanese army? You Palestinians are nothing in Lebanon now. Do you think anyone will listen?'

Despite my terror, I tried to stay outwardly calm.

'I am a nurse and I have to report to the director of the hospital about what happens during my shift. This murder happened on my shift and of course I reported it.'

I suggested they ask the Lebanese hospital administrator why he had sent the report to the PLO and to ask the PLO why it had sent the report to them. At that point one of the officers started to swear at me and demanded, 'Why did you refuse to come here yesterday?'

'I have learned from my father to be sure of my situation, especially with government officials and people in the army, and to be strong. I wanted to be sure the Italians knew where we were.' I went on to tell him that, as a Palestinian in Lebanon, I was protected by the UN and, at this time, by the Italians in the camp.

One of the officers started to threaten me, saying he wanted to take revenge against all Palestinians and that he would kill us all. It was by now a familiar threat, but I still felt my knees go weak and my throat tighten in fear. I clasped my hands together tightly to stop them shaking. Another officer said menacingly, 'Poor Palestinian, you have no power, you are still young, you should not be involved in any politics'.

I replied that I was not involved in any politics and I was only doing what I had been asked to do by the hospital's Lebanese administrator. I was then given a strong but threatening lecture. 'Take care, because now you are under our thumb. If we find out you are involved in politics, we will hang you where they buried all the people who were massacred in Sabra and Shatila.' Then they let me go.

Outside, I trembled uncontrollably, quickly finding a place to sit, fearing I might fall. I remembered my Uncle Muhamad who had been taken by the Lebanese security in 1962, tortured and murdered. At the time he had been in charge of field services for UNRWA, but that did not protect him. He, like so many, had died struggling for justice for my people.

The period between mid-September and December 1982 was truly terrible for all the refugees in the camps. We were never safe, and young men were especially vulnerable. The Lebanese army, often accompanied by the Lebanese Christian Forces, entered the camps many times, taking any boys aged over 13. They would arrest them for no reason, order them to take off their shirts and then beat them where they stood. Many were taken away in trucks, never to be seen again.

Not long after the murder of Nawal's brother was the feast of Eid al-Adha. This was the first Muslim feast day after Israel had invaded Lebanon. As was our custom, my parents and many elderly people left Burj Barajneh early in the morning to go to the nearby cemetery to remember the dead. Young people, who generally do not go on such visits, stayed behind. On the way back, these elderly camp residents were confronted by the Lebanese army and forbidden to re-enter the camp. The army began to search the camp, taking all the young men they could find.

As with everything done to us, most of these searches were carried out in a vicious manner. In a previous search a neighbour's house had been ransacked and all her mattresses slashed. On this day, however, a young soldier went to the house of my Aunt Amina, my mother's young sister. When my aunt saw that he was wearing a cross, she became very frightened, although she did not have teenage boys; and her children were only young. She opened the cupboard and started to take out all the sheets, having seen what had been done in our neighbour's house.

'No, no, don't take anything out,' the soldier remonstrated. 'I am sorry to come into your house, but this is an order and I am in the army. Your baby is asleep, so let him sleep. Just let me stay for five minutes or so, otherwise if the officer sees me enter your house and come out quickly, I will be in trouble. So, let us sit here together.'

My aunt was amazed; she had been prepared for the worst. We knew that not all Lebanese soldiers and not all Christians hated the Palestinians. This young man showed respect for us as human beings. Before leaving, he apologised to my aunt and soon after, left the house.

That day, I was working at Gaza Hospital when I heard that the Lebanese army was in Burj camp. I was deeply concerned for my brothers Ihab, who we also call Abu Khalil, and Amer, who was just 15. I knew my parents were at the cemetery and my brothers were at home. Although more than 600 young people were taken that day, my brothers were lucky; the army missed them. Many women, mostly those who were in the women's union and active in the community, were among those taken. During this period, thousands of Palestinians and Lebanese were arrested and held in shocking conditions in detention. Most were not charged, but beatings and torture were common. Included in this campaign of summary actions was my 25-year-old brother, Abu Khalil, who in early April 1983, was taken and held for six months during which he was tortured. On a daily basis, whenever I came home, I did not know if my father and my brothers would be there or if they had been taken prisoner. It was a very insecure time.

The Multinational Force peacekeepers around our camp tried to stop the beatings and arrests. But I remember one incident when a young boy, not more than 12 or so, was arrested, just outside the hospital and in front of a number of us who were walking to work. A Lebanese army officer forcibly removed the boy's shirt and started beating him with a belt. The Italians, who were on patrol nearby, were furious and intervened. While they stopped this particular beating, they were unable to stop all the arrests and killings. The 20,000 or so Palestinians, mostly those ethnically cleansed from East Beirut and squatting, unprotected, in buildings around the city, were particularly vulnerable during these months. And moving from Beirut to Damascus or to the south was dangerous, too, with the Christian Lebanese Forces militia sharing checkpoints with the Israelis. We did not have any camp leaders: anyone could come at will into the camp. There was no PLO, and no fighters. We were as totally unprotected as we had been before 1969.

◈◈◈

It was in the middle of this crisis that I met another Australian, Helen McCue. She came to Gaza Hospital about 10 days after the Sabra massacre. I was busy in the emergency ward attending to the daily toll. A little boy had picked up a cluster bomb made in the shape of a toy and had taken it to his house in Shatila camp where he had dropped it, killing himself and seriously injuring his mother who was pregnant, and his two sisters. The unborn baby had died and both the mother and one of the boy's sisters lost a leg as well. I was busy dealing with the boy's family when a nurse came to tell me there was a foreigner waiting for me outside. Helen introduced herself and told me she was a volunteer nurse teacher who had come at the suggestion of Dr Said Dyjani, head of the PRCS School of Nursing in Damascus, to help rebuild the nursing team in the wake of the massacre. He had also suggested she contact me as he knew my English was good, and that she also contact Umm Walid, the head of the PRCS in Lebanon at that time.

When we met Umm Walid, she agreed the PRCS school should be reopened as soon as possible and also agreed with Dr Dyjani that we needed to train nurses. A number of PRCS staff, among them nurses, had been wounded and killed during the Israeli invasion so there was an urgent need for replacements. She suggested that with the school of nursing at Akka Hospital still in ruins, we start with a nurse in-service training program at Gaza Hospital. She also suggested I work with Helen and help her with the translation for this program. Over the next six months, working together day and night, Helen and I became close friends. During the morning we were involved in the nurse in-service training, and in the afternoons and evenings we worked on the hospital wards. At that time there were still many people in the hospital recovering from shocking wounds suffered in the Sabra and Shatila massacre. There were also many false alerts that Christian Lebanese Forces were entering the camps slaughtering people again. These rumours would send people fleeing to the hospital for safety, terrified of another massacre.

On one occasion, I had to go to the south of Lebanon to visit relatives in Rashidyyeh camp, and I took Helen along. The trip was quite stressful, as there were many Israeli checkpoints, but fortunately, we had no trouble. On our return trip, we stopped in Sidon and went together to what remained of the Ain al Helwah refugee camp, which had previously housed more than 30,000 people. It had been literally flattened during the war and was now just a huge dusty field. Where had all the camp residents gone? We found a few women and children huddling together in an open shelter that had only three walls and a battered tin roof full of bullet holes. As they told us their story of loss and disaster, we both stood there, numb and speechless. I muttered what words of comfort I could find. Then Helen and I walked away, tears pouring down our cheeks. But my grief soon turned to anger, and outside the hearing of these poor women, I exploded in a rage at this devastation before us.

◈◈◈

In December, I began to prepare my papers to take up a scholarship in England funded by UNIPAL, a British charity that organised educational exchanges. This was a long and complicated process since, as a Palestinian refugee, I had no citizenship or nationality, so therefore, no passport. We did have a UN refugee identity document, but that was only valid for travel inside Lebanon, and even that was restricted. So, getting my visa took many months and much support from Mrs Moore, my teacher at the PRCS School of Nursing.

Meanwhile, Helen and I continued working together until March 1983, when the Lebanese government started to deport all foreigners working with the Palestinians. Not wanting to be deported, Helen decided to return to Australia, but promised it would not be the last time we saw each other. I remember her words very clearly: 'I am working alone now but I want to go back to Australia and get more people involved, and then Olfat, dear, we can support your people more effectively.'

That same month, I left for my eight-month training program in London.

11

A TASTE OF FREEDOM

Landing at Heathrow Airport was like arriving on another planet. As I emerged from customs, a sea of humanity greeted me. The differences were instantly obvious—everyone spoke English for a start. But it was more than that—shops were overflowing with goods, the place was clean, the walls had no bullet holes and there were no soldiers. But there was also no Mrs Moore.

In retrospect, it was not surprising. My original flight was over-booked so I had been bumped to a flight the following day. Because of my inexperience in such matters, I had somehow assumed Mrs Moore would realise what had happened and still be there. A few phone calls later and I realised not only was Mrs Moore not coming, she had left London for a few days—expecting me on the same flight the following week. I was on my own. It was late, and I began to grow anxious about what to do next. However, in true Arabic style a young Lebanese student I had met on the plane offered me a place for the night at her sister's house.

As we drove from the airport in their car, a wave of new images kept me alert and fascinated. The road was smooth, not filled with the huge potholes and bomb craters I was used to swerving around. The traffic lights worked, and all the drivers obeyed them. The buildings were tall, ordered and intact, and there was an extraordinary sense of social order. But most striking of all was the fact that there were no checkpoints, no menacing soldiers, no militia. For the first time in my adult life I experienced a sense of safety and order.

The next day, I remembered I had been given the phone number of a friend of a British nurse I had worked with in Lebanon. I called, and to my delight, my friend answered the phone—it turned out all the foreign staff had been evicted from Lebanon, which was why my plane was overbooked.

'So, you are the reason I have this problem now!' I said, laughing.

Luckily, I was able to stay with her and her friends until my course at Cambridge started; and was delighted to find she lived in a building with a group of students from Palestine. These were the first Palestinians I'd ever met who had actually been living in my homeland. In Lebanon, we were isolated from our people in Palestine—we knew, of course, about the political events taking place there, but had no idea what life was actually like. Nor did they know what life was like in the camps in Lebanon. It was exhilarating to meet my own people who were living in that almost mythical land we, in the camps, had only ever dreamed of. We talked and talked. They told me about life in Palestine and how hard it was, that the occupying Israeli army controlled every aspect of their lives. Even for them as students in London, it was risky to speak too freely. I later learned that when they graduated and returned to occupied Palestine, many were detained and interrogated, and some were imprisoned.

That first week also brought another revelation when the parents of one of the students visited, bringing olives and labneh from my homeland. I could smell my land in these good people and the food they carried. This was the first time I had eaten food from the soil of Palestine, and even now I can taste it and remember well the sense of longing it evoked in me.

My changed circumstances really became apparent on my second night when we went to the movies. As everyone was preparing to leave, I began searching for my refugee identity papers, and was astonished when they told me I wouldn't need them. It had become second nature to me to carry my identity card to get through military checkpoints. In London, I understood for the first time what freedom meant; I was being treated as a human being, able to go anywhere I wanted, unheeded. It was such an exhilarating feeling—yet all I was really experiencing was a normal life. After this wonderful introduction to London, I spent a month in Cambridge getting used to the language and doing some voluntary work in a hospital for two hours a day. From Cambridge, I went to a nursing school in Epping, north-east of London, and then on to observe clinical teaching in the local hospital.

My first few months in England were filled with new experiences. I was constantly comparing things in London with things in Lebanon. In London, with all the freedom and all the civil rights people took for granted, I began to understand our predicament more fully and feel more acutely my own, and my people's, lack of rights. My stay in England was a glorious experience, but my work in English hospitals really highlighted the deprivation we suffered. To come from Gaza Hospital in the camp where everything was old and damaged by the war, to hospitals with excellent facilities was a real shock. One of the things that particularly struck me in the hospital was a special type of chair they used to carry patients to the bathroom and to lift them into and out of the bath or shower recess. After the war, there were many severely disabled people in Gaza Hospital and we had to struggle to carry and lift patients by hand—a very painful experience for the patients and a great strain on the nurses. Working in these English hospitals, with all their wonderful facilities, was for me like stepping into a futuristic world. Yet in reality, the equipment was just standard fare—it was just in Lebanon we were used to working with no resources.

There were so many positive things to learn. I liked the idea of having social workers in hospital to deal with patients' social and psychological problems. But some of these 'problems' were difficult for me to relate to. I remember one patient who was deeply concerned about her four cats being left alone at home. The social worker was brought in and arranged for someone to go to this woman's house, pick up the cats and take them to a cattery. We love animals, too, but this simple act on the social worker's part astounded me. I remember thinking, 'Oh my God, people care so much about cats and dogs while we live in miserable camps where people can slaughter and kill us, where no one values human life. In England the cats and dogs are cared for more than Palestinian refugees in camps in Lebanon.'

To come from my camp home—where nine children had lived in a single tiny room, where we had a minute kitchen, leaking waste water and, of course, no garden—to the nurses' home in Epping where I was now staying, with its many rooms and toilets and nice garden, initially overwhelmed me. I raged, inwardly, especially lying in bed at night, asking myself why we had to live as we did in Lebanon, exiled from our ancestral home. My parents had come from a financially secure background; they'd been affluent and had owned land and houses. Now we lived in dreadful poverty, in a miserable camp, in daily fear of our lives; a situation not of our making. Indeed, while I was in England, it often crossed my mind that the British were responsible for our situation in the first place. But what kept me going through my first week or so at the nursing school was the clear objective I had: I was in the UK to learn as much as possible and to take that knowledge back to my people.

Although the teachers were a great help and I coped reasonably well with my work, I found the loneliness of my off-duty hours particularly difficult to bear. There were five rooms in my corridor in the nurses' home and a shared bathroom, toilet and kitchen. Occasionally, I would see other students, who would smile, but do nothing more; there were no offers to share a cup of tea or a chat. After finishing tuition in the afternoon, I'd be in my room until eight o'clock the next morning, alone with my books and the silence. Coming from a culture where everyone talks to one other, where we are hospitable and share everything, I thought I was going to die from all that loneliness and silence.

I desperately needed to speak to someone so at every opportunity, I visited my Palestinian friends in London. Mostly the train journey was straightforward, but one evening they invited me to join them about five hours outside London. Once again, a friend's family was visiting from Palestine. They'd bought fresh *mulukhiya* (a leafy green vegetable) and were making *bisarah*, a dish cooked with dried beans, lots of garlic and usually served semi-solid on a plate. It is very popular in summer and, as it is a vegetarian dish, it is my very favourite Palestinian food. The train journey took four hours. My friends met me at the station and I had dinner with them. Afterwards, because I had to be back at the nursing school for the morning, I went straight back. Eight hours of train travel, just for *bisarah*! But it was worth it.

I had been in Epping for 10 days when there was finally a knock on my door. When I opened it, a sweet Irish student called Kerry introduced herself. When I told her that she was the first person to really talk to me at the school, she laughed and said, 'Don't worry, that's the English for you. They're very nice really, and eventually you'll get to like them, but it takes time! I had the same problem when I came here—and I speak the same language.'

We soon became good friends. One long weekend she invited me to her home in Northern Ireland. After we'd sorted out the visa issue, which took some time, I spent four wonderful days with her family; and quickly realised the Irish and the Palestinians had many things in common. When her mum made sweets, she gave Kerry a plate to take to a neighbour, and the neighbour in turn brought food to them. When we walked in the street, people would say hello to us. These neighbourly gestures and public greetings were redolent of our culture, too, and I felt welcomed and at home for the first time since arriving in the UK. On another occasion Kerry took me to a pub. When the locals found out I was Palestinian, I was instantly the star attraction and treated almost like a PLO leader. As they hugged me with their laughter and warmth, they told me they loved the Palestinians because they, the people of Northern Ireland, understood oppression and occupation. They were fighting for their independence, too, they said. It was a marvellous few hours of solidarity.

On one of the days of my visit, the family decided to take me into southern Ireland. I was worried because I didn't have a visa for that country, but Kerry was quite relaxed about it all. 'Don't worry,' she said. 'At the border they only ask for the car registration papers, not visas.' Still I remained anxious. As we approached the border checkpoint, a familiar fear rose in my body, and all the feelings of anger and humiliation I'd experienced at similar checkpoints in my life came flooding back. Armed police hovered in the background and snipers were hidden behind brick towers that loomed above the road. I sat tense and rigid while the border guards checked the car registration papers. My relief was profound when we drove safely through. Kerry looked at me and laughed, 'See, Olfat. No problem.' Unlike Kerry, I knew as a Palestinian I'd be treated differently if my documents had been checked. Nevertheless, I relaxed quickly and was able to laugh, too.

At a local festival in the south, thousands of people were out celebrating, the sound of music and singing spilling out on the street as hard to resist as an ocean wave. As I watched them I hoped we, too, might one day be able to celebrate like that. It struck me that this was the first time I'd seen so many people together looking so happy. I'd taken part in big demonstrations in Lebanon, but they were usually electric with anger and fear. But here were people singing, dancing and laughing. Here were stalls laden with food and beautiful things to buy. It was wonderful. I bought a small wooden object that looked like a hammer and had the words for 'good luck' written on it in Gaelic. I held it close and hoped for better times for my people. This lovely day was one of the highlights of my happy stay in Ireland.

Although my time in England was generally a good experience, I faced some frustrations. UNIPAL hadn't made any plans for me to formally address public meetings. This disappointed me because it meant we'd lost an opportunity to spread the word about our plight as Palestinian refugees in Lebanon. Though I often spent pleasant weekends with UNIPAL people and would talk as much as possible to students, teachers and others in the nursing school about our situation, I felt this wasn't enough. I wanted to tell many more people about life in the refugee camps. After I'd had one of my informal talks in the hospital, Nina Syrial, one of the psychologists there, phoned me in the nurses' home.

'Olfat, I was shocked to hear you speaking about Palestine as your homeland,' she said. 'I always thought the Jewish people were fighting the Palestinians because it was they who'd taken the land from the Jewish people, not the other way around. When you said your grandparents had been born in Palestine, and your mother too, I thought that you were lying.'

I was a little taken aback by this and began to go over the historical facts with her again. But she interrupted me.

'After your talk, I went to the library where my sister works and asked for a pre-1948 world map. When I looked for Israel I found Palestine.'

Nina told me she was shattered to find out how ignorant she'd been and how she'd accepted information without question. She'd always believed people when they'd told her Israel was for Jewish people and the Palestinians wanted to take it from them. She'd never heard that Palestinians had been exiled from their ancestral land. I wasn't surprised about her misunderstanding, but I was deeply saddened all the same. The need to educate people about our situation, our rights as refugees and our struggle to go home became even more apparent.

I returned to my life as a Palestinian refugee in Lebanon in December 1983. I had been away eight months, but it felt as if I had lived a whole new life. Yet in Lebanon the old life had continued as it always had—with war and death. Fierce fighting had continued in my absence. On one side was Israel, supported by the US, and at the same time supporting the Lebanese Christian Forces; on the other was Syria, backed by the Soviet Union, supporting the Lebanese leftist alliance, which included Muslim as well as Christian political and militia groups. Amal, a nationalist and mostly Shi'a leftist militia in West Beirut, had also entered the fray. And in the south, a growing body of Islamist Shi'a had formed the militant Hezbollah (Party of God) faction, which was backed by Iran. In West Beirut the Lebanese army continued to harass the Palestinians who had been disarmed since 1982. The US-sponsored Multinational Force (MNF) was still supporting the Lebanese government and had poured considerable resources into building up the army and training new recruits, mainly Shi'a. But the Lebanese army command remained dominated by ex-Lebanese Forces men. It was a recipe for continued conflict.

During my time in England, attacks against US and French troops had increased. Throughout September there were multiple attacks on both the French and US military by the Islamic Jihad Organisation, culminating in the October 19 suicide bombings that killed 241 US marines and 57 French soldiers in attacks on their barracks in Beirut. For those nations, it was the last straw and by February 1984 the US marines and French MNF troops had pulled out of Beirut. The battle for control of the city began again in earnest.

The Lebanese army attacked Lebanese Shi'a areas once more, causing considerable consternation in its own ranks. Nabih Berri, leader of Amal, now well armed by the Syrians, persuaded 60 per cent of the Lebanese army's recruits, mostly Shi'a, to defect. Its numbers thus seriously depleted, the Lebanese army was routed from West Beirut. The US-brokered peace plan was in tatters, and Syrian and Israeli withdrawal talks had stalled. Beirut was once more divided, with Muslim Shi'a, Druze and leftist militia forces in the west, and the Christian Lebanese Forces back in the east.

As in the past, most of the fighting was concentrated along the Green Line. The Israelis occupied Southern Lebanon, and the Syrians were in the Beqaa Valley. Lebanon was thus fractured into four cantons. There had been civil war for nine years, hundreds of thousands of Lebanese and Palestinians had been killed and wounded, and the country was shattered and anarchic. Ironically for us, however, this upheaval for Lebanon was a time of peace for Palestinians in the country as it took attention away from the camps—with the Lebanese army leaving us relatively alone.

On my return from England, I began teaching at the Palestinian Red Cross School of Nursing in Beirut but realised that I faced a major problem: all our teaching resources—anatomical models, diagrams and nursing library—had been destroyed. Without these facilities, passing on the experience and knowledge I'd gained in the UK to the students proved very challenging. Still, I did my best, and we made some progress.

Like so many other Palestinians, my family was busy repairing their house, and the rest of their time was focused on the hardest of jobs—survival. As always, my grandfather continued growing food for his family; he was happiest when he was out working the land. As his children grew and got jobs, they urged him to stop his work, insisting his sons could now care for the family. But my grandfather would always refuse saying he would die of unhappiness if he couldn't continue to work the land.

On February 6, 1984, my grandfather failed to come home from work. We contacted the landowner in case my grandfather had gone to see him, as he often did. But he wasn't there. We then went to all the hospitals nearby, fearing the worst. Since the Amal militia dominated the area, we asked for their help. The fields where my grandfather worked were near the airport, in no-man's land. But not even Amal could get in there at night; it was far too dangerous.

None of us could sleep that night. We imagined him alone in that open space, perhaps sick or injured, or even dead. In the morning an Amal officer came to our house and told us our grandfather was in a nearby hospital. He had died alone in his fields. When we went to see him, we found a clump of grass and soil clutched in his right hand. Seeing that he wasn't wounded, we concluded he must have died from a heart attack. We were especially distressed that he'd died alone, and that his body had lain outside for the entire night without any member of the family to tend it; but were comforted by the thought he'd died with grass and his beloved soil in his hand. We knew this land had given him strength, as had the land of Palestine.

Thirty-six years after he had fled the Israeli attack on his home in the Galilee, Abu Ahmad died a refugee, an exile. We buried him in the Palestinian camp cemetery near Mar Elias, far from his beloved Tarshiha.

12

DOWN UNDER

During my time in England I'd kept in touch with my friend, Helen McCue. By January 1984, true to her word, she'd formed the Australian People for Health Education and Development Abroad (APHEDA) with the help of Cliff Dolan, president of the Australian Council of Trade Unions (ACTU). APHEDA became the ACTU's overseas aid arm.[22] Its first aim was to initiate health care and vocational training for refugees in camps such as those in Lebanon. Helen had also been able to raise money for various Palestinian nurse-training projects in Lebanon and Palestine.

Helen returned to Beirut in April 1984 to select candidates for short courses in Australia in community nursing and other areas of clinical nursing. In the end the successful applicants were two male and four female nurses from Lebanon and two female nurses from UNRWA—one from Gaza and the other from Jordan. Because my English was good, I was appointed the group's spokesperson and translator. When I told my father I was going, he was, of course, delighted. He surprised me by telling me that he had thought about migrating to Australia in the late 1950s to escape the civil war. As

---

22 APHEDA now known as Union Aid Abroad-APHEDA

an accountant with good English and a young family, he believed he could make a good life in that country, but his mother had begged him not to go as he was her only son left in Lebanon. How my life would have been different if he had taken that journey.

Having only UN refugee documents, my fellow Palestinian nurses and I faced mountainous visa problems and extraordinary travel restrictions. We finally flew to Australia in September 1984. At a stopover in the Persian Gulf, Palestinians on the flight weren't allowed to leave the airport building, though the other passengers had a good night's sleep in a hotel. We arrived in Australia exhausted after the long flight but excited nonetheless. Our language skills were improved by a month-long, English course with Donna Burns and other volunteer teachers. During our six months in Australia, three members of our group, including myself, were placed in community health centres; while the rest gained experience in various hospitals in Sydney. It was an incredible learning curve; and working in the community seemed a much better fit for our camp situation, and something I could help establish back in Lebanon.

However, it was the second arm of my work in Australia that really inspired me. As part of APHEDA's advocacy work for refugees, I'd agreed to combine my nursing work with community education about the Palestinian refugee situation. I'd brought a video and photos, and during my visits to different health centres, I was able to hold small informal sessions talking to people about our life and our health care work in the camps. I ran one of these sessions for staff at an inner-Sydney youth community centre where I spent a week. After I'd finished my talk, a young doctor in the audience angrily accused me of lying. He seemed particularly upset about my account of the Sabra and Shatila massacre. I told him I wasn't lying, that all the facts were well documented, and my photos and video were entirely authentic. He wasn't placated and remained angry, although the other nurses said they'd heard and seen the news about our situation and the massacre, so didn't doubt me.

The next day the doctor refused to speak to me. On my third day at the centre, he called me to his room where he was interviewing a teenager. After he'd finished, he discussed the details of the case with me. Then he offered me coffee. As we sat and drank our coffee, he brought up the subject of my talk.

'You know, Olfat, it wasn't easy for me to accept what you told us the other day,' he said. 'Since then I've been quite distressed so I visited my mother to ask her about Palestine.'

The doctor's mother had confirmed everything I'd said. It was then that he revealed he was Jewish and that it had been difficult for him to believe me. He was gracious enough to apologise for being rude.

It was a painful encounter for both of us, but we ended up respecting each other's position. He was a fine doctor and I understood that the facts of history are sometimes distorted. I understood, too, that facing the truth could sometimes be painful. Being an effective spokesperson for my people in public forums, and especially in another country, was fulfilling and deeply rewarding after all my years of feeling helpless and silenced within the tiny confines of our camp and my workplace. APHEDA organised many public functions where our group could talk to Australians about the Palestinian plight. Helen would ring me and say, 'Olfat, there's a meeting I want you to attend. Never mind that you're not prepared; just say what you know and what's in your heart.'

There were some confronting moments, of course. The week after we arrived in Australia, we held a press conference. Dressed in black blouses with traditional embroidery and our black and white *keffiyeh* draped around our shoulders or covering our heads, we were ready to represent our people. I was taken aback, though, when a journalist asked, 'If Israel wanted to give blood to the Palestinians, would you accept it?'

After a moment's thought, I said, 'If they offered us blood I would ask them to stop the bombing so that we wouldn't need to spill so much blood in the first place.'

The other journalists clapped at my response and a surge of pride pulsed through me like a shot of adrenalin. This was my first press conference and I felt I'd represented my people well.

Another time we travelled as a group to Melbourne to address a large gathering of trade unionists. Helen gave a speech about APHEDA and then I spoke about the Palestinian situation. When we'd finished, a trade unionist stood up and asked, 'How can you guarantee that any material assistance we send will not be damaged by the war?'

My first reaction was indignation: the question implied that equipment was more important than our lives. I understood the need to be accountable, but how could we provide a guarantee of security in a war situation.

'If I cannot guarantee my life, how can you expect me to guarantee your donated equipment and your machines? But we need this assistance desperately, and we will do what we can to guarantee its proper use.'

The opportunities I had to put the Palestinian cause in Australia gave me great confidence and helped me find my voice and become an effective public speaker. When I was young, my father used to tell me I had a strong personality. While I was in Australia, I felt for the first time that I had the opportunity to express that personality in public in a way that helped my people. It was an experience that shaped and influenced me enormously.

◈◈◈

On the day I returned from Australia, April 11, 1985, my neighbour, a young male named Ahmed, was shot and killed in the street outside the camp. There were a number of what seemed to be random assassinations like these in and around the camp, but none of us knew who was responsible. There were no armed Palestinians in the camp, and West Beirut was under the military control of the Shi'a Amal Movement, who we considered our friends. We all lived in the same neighbourhood and I had gone to school with many of the young men who were in this Amal Movement. So, it is no surprise we were ill-prepared for what later happened.

Within a month of my return, Lebanon's Palestinians again became the focus of a power struggle between the different religious sects and ideological factions in that war-torn country. When the French created the modern boundaries of Lebanon in the 1920s, the Shi'a community was located in the south of the country, some areas of East Beirut and the Beqaa Valley. They were generally an impoverished, rural community but with strong religious links to the Shi'a in southern Iraq and in Iran. During the time of Lebanon's economic growth in the 1950s and 60s, they were economically marginalised. In the 1970s, Imam Mousa Sadr emerged to lead the Lebanese Shi'a in the Movement of the Deprived (Harakat al Mahrumeen). Its military arm, Amal, was formed in 1974 and supported the Palestinian struggle for liberation. But by the end of the 1970s, concern was growing that the predominantly Sunni Palestinians might stay and that this population would increase Sunni numbers in Lebanon, thereby impacting on the country's 'confessional' system where power is distributed proportionally among religious sects.

During the Israeli siege of Beirut in 1982, Amal fought alongside the Lebanese and Palestinian resistance and by February 1984 this coalition was able to expel the Lebanese army and Lebanese Forces militia from West Beirut, leaving Amal as the dominant militia in West Beirut and the south. The Palestinians in the Beirut camps were unarmed and defenceless but had no cause to believe Amal would attack them.

On May 18, 1985 I was returning home from Gaza Hospital and as I approached Burj camp I saw it was surrounded by sandbags as if in preparation for an attack. When I got home my mother was greatly relieved.

'Something's wrong,' she said. 'Amal have put sandbags all around the camp.'

At that time there were no fighters in the camp. My father who with other men, had formed a popular committee to support our community, went to Amal and asked why it was putting up sandbags around the camp. On his return he reassured us of Amal's good intentions.

'Amal leaders said that, as tomorrow is the start of Ramadan and often there are clashes at this time, they are expecting an attack by the Lebanese Forces. They are getting ready to protect us in case of this attack.'

In the morning I woke at 6 o'clock as usual and headed off to work. As I walked past the big square in the camp I saw my younger brother Amer, then 17 years. 'Why are you going to the hospital,' he asked me. 'Haven't you heard the news?'

He told me Gaza Hospital had been occupied by Amal who had killed many of those inside. I was totally shocked. I could not believe Amal would do that; I raced home and tuned into the Lebanese Forces radio station. The first news item detailed the Gaza Hospital occupation and an attack on Sabra and Shatila. The announcer talked about 'Palestinian terrorists', and that all Palestinians should be forced out of Lebanon. It was a familiar theme. But we were shocked and surprised by the news of this attack as we all knew there were no fighters in the camps. All of the camps in Beirut were under the political control of Palestinian groups aligned to Syria and of no threat whatsoever to the Lebanese. These Amal fighters were our neighbours; we went to school with them. How could they do this and why? None of us could believe what we heard.

After hearing this news, my mother quickly left the camp to buy bread; we feared the worst, so wanted to stock up. On her return she told us everything appeared normal outside: there were many people walking around, shopping and going about their daily business. Then as she spoke, without warning, heavy shooting erupted on the edge of the camp, with a concentration on our Tarshiha area. Like my mother, many people had been out shopping and were caught by surprise. We had no defence, no weapons and no one to fight for us. Soon after, Amer rushed into the house. When he saw me he said, 'Why are you sitting here, Olfat, what is wrong with you? Why aren't you at the hospital?

'First, you tell me not to go to work, and now you come and say I should be at work. What is the matter with you? Didn't you hear the news that Gaza Hospital is occupied?'

'No, no Olfat,' he said, 'I am not talking about Gaza Hospital. I'm talking about Haifa Hospital, here in our camp. It is full of dead and wounded.'

I noticed, then, that he was covered in blood.

'What has happened to you?'

He told me his friend Banil Farise, a neighbour from Tarshiha, had been killed. Banil had taken leave from his work in Saudi Arabia to visit his family during Ramadan and was killed as he was running through the camp when the shooting started. Amer had been with him and had brought him to the hospital.

'Olfat, it is shocking,' Amer said. 'You must go now.'

We both left for the hospital immediately, sprinting through the camp's narrow alleys. The heavy shooting continued. We were careful when we came to areas where we knew Amal snipers could see us from their vantage points in the tall apartment buildings on the edge of the camp. In a few minutes we had arrived at the hospital. By this time it was 11 o'clock but even before I entered the main entrance hall I could hear the crying and wailing.

Before me was a nightmarish scene. There were bodies and blood everywhere. More than 100 dead and wounded lay there with family members beside them. I had already been through many years of war, but never had I encountered such carnage. There were young boys, children and women, all screaming and crying, blood covering their heads or abdominal wounds. Some had shattered limbs in grotesque positions. Relatives were quietly praying, others were crying out for help. Scattered among the wounded were people who were obviously dead. It was an unbelievable and indescribable scene of human suffering. Struggling, I overcame my numbness and carefully stepped through the bodies to the overflowing emergency room.

On entering, Walid, one of the nurses on duty, said, 'Thank God, you were here in the camp! Yalla (let's move). We do not have any other trained nurses; there are only assistant nurses and first-aid workers.'

We faced an immediate critical decision about how to manage this crisis. Haifa was not a hospital; it was only a rehabilitation centre with a few polyclinics. There was no emergency centre or operating theatre and only a small pharmacy with nothing of substance to help us with this catastrophe. The doctors who attended the clinics lived outside the camp and, as it was early, they had not yet arrived; and later, when they tried were turned back. A young doctor recently graduated from Romania was with us, but he was not very experienced in this type of emergency work. Walid, a few of the nurses, Salim, the nurse administrator, and I, had had many years of war experience, but even we were overwhelmed. Naidal, the hospital administrator, and the secretary Khaireyah, were there to help us too.

Several members of the camp's popular committee had arrived at the same time as I had, so together we planned what to do. First, we dispatched people to find out what resources we actually had in the hospital; and to call for volunteers and for people to bring first-aid materials they might have in their homes. Then, while one of the committee members tried desperately to contact the Red Cross to help us, Walid and I started to triage the wounded and confirm the dead.

We quickly identified those we thought might survive with the help of our meagre resources and the nurses set to making them comfortable. The small number of beds available and were quickly filled so we covered the floor with mattresses for the rest.

It took until 4 p.m. to open a large room and put all the fatally wounded on mattresses in that room. Though we felt sickened and overwhelmed, we knew there was nothing we could do for them having no access to medical supplies that could help, no doctors, and no operating room or resuscitation equipment. I struggled inwardly as we helped these poor people and their families into this relatively quiet space so they could die with a semblance of dignity.

Having identified the dead, we opened another large room as a temporary mortuary. We covered the bodies with lime, hoping we could eventually make arrangements for them to be buried but this was difficult, too, as no one could go to the nearby cemetery due to the heavy fighting. People were crying and grieving, while we tried desperately to calm them.

◈◈◈

I cannot explain how I felt that day. It felt as if a part of me died in that moment. Never before had I been faced with such a shocking dilemma. I felt terribly guilty; who was I to decide these critical matters as to who we should treat first; who we should save. It was sickening making such life and death decisions knowing that every moment counted. I had dealt with many things, but I had always been able to help the wounded, to do something. And now for the first time in my life, there was nothing I could do for my people. I knew when we put the critically wounded in that large room, that they would die; and it was heartbreaking knowing these people would have survived if we'd had some facilities and trained doctors. I struggled to control my own emotions in the midst of all of these grieving relatives and their loss. At the end of the day I was exhausted; but the fighting continued, unrelentingly. I was filled with despair, with great sadness and sick with worry about my family and all the camp residents.

One victim that day was a young boy with a severe head injury. The only thing we had for emergency respiration was a manual air bag. We showed his mother how to use it. As she worked the bag she prayed over her dying child. She laboured for about eight hours before he died. Many people died that day who only needed a small operation, but we had no anaesthetics, no doctors, nothing.

Through the camp walkie-talkie we contacted the PRCS in Mar Elias camp. The PRCS called the Red Cross but nobody came; the Amal militia would not allow them to enter the camp, even to take our wounded. For me, this was a doubly traumatic time, not only because of the number of casualties on that first day but because all the people who were brought in wounded or dead were my neighbours and friends. They were from the Tarshiha area of the camp, people

I knew very well. I was expecting at any moment to see my mother, my sisters or my brothers brought in wounded and bleeding or dead. Nabil Faris, our neighbour's only able son, was dead when I went to the hospital. Another neighbour, Dogman, the only boy in the family—recently married, his wife pregnant—was brought in dead. Muhammad Ara, who had carried Dogman to the hospital in the hope he could be saved, was later brought back himself, shot dead. Neighbour after neighbour, every few minutes. I fought down a rising sense of panic as yet another wounded person arrived. I could not bear it. Inside, I cried for all of them.

To make things worse, we had no leaders in the camp. The PLO—its fighters and the leadership—had left Beirut in 1982. The only community leaders we had were older men such as my father. There were no guns, no fighters, nothing with which we could protect ourselves. In the first few hours of fighting more than 10 young people with no military experience were killed and many wounded as they tried helplessly to defend the camp. The older men were not military leaders but felt they needed to try and save the camp. One of these men, who back in 1967 had been involved in al-Fatah, happened to be in the camp visiting relatives for Ramadan. He was also from Tarshiha. When he heard about the attack, he immediately went to the mosque and, via the loudspeaker normally used to call people to prayer, told the camp residents to stay in their homes and take shelter. He then called all the young men together to organise a self-defence system with a plan to protect the camp's perimeter as he realised this was no one-day attack.

Before the Israeli invasion of 1982, the PLO had a maintenance department that cleaned and serviced weapons. Three men who worked in that department were still in the camp, so they were charged with making weapons to protect the camp with whatever was to hand. Women collected cans and nails and brought petrol to the team of men from which small bombs could be made that could be thrown by hand. Women also made sandbags using blankets and sheets that they filled with soil.

Initially, many of the young men protecting the camp entrances suffered serious head, neck and chest wounds, as there were only the sandbags to protect them. Also, as they stood to throw the hand-made bombs they could be hit. Later, when Amal realised that they could not enter the camp with impunity, they attacked with tanks and artillery. By then we were a little more prepared. The under-ground shelters had been cleaned and people were hiding in the lower storeys of their houses. Usually the shelling would die down around 3 a.m. after which, I deemed it reasonably safe to go home from the hospital to shower and change my clothes. Still, at this late hour, I would find my mother, my grandmother and my aunt sitting on the floor with their faces in their hands, waiting, terrified that one of their own would be killed or wounded. My aunt and my grandmother had left their houses to come and stay with my family. My aunt's house was on the border of the camp and while our house was also close to the border, it was marginally safer. With my aunt's family, my grandmother, my brother's family-in-law and all of my family, there were 28 people living in two small rooms. We could not use the upstairs rooms because they had been severely damaged, but also, that section of the house was very exposed to artillery fire.

People were crammed into every corner of the house. We had no electricity and we had to hand collect water when we could. We were only able to wash our bodies with a small jug of water once a week. Of course, no clothes were washed. There was only one small toilet. We ran out of detergent quickly and, one time I came home to see my mother using my best and favourite perfume just to try and erase the smell in the toilet.

As the attack turned into a month-long siege, food became a problem. There were few shops in the camp and no room for vegetable gardens. People soon began to starve. Some lactating women did not have enough food to produce milk, so many babies died during these weeks. Based on her experiences over the years, my mother, however, had a habit of stockpiling dried foods such as rice, bourghul, lentils, onions, oil, and gas for the stove, so that unlike many others, we were able to have one meal a day. While there were no fresh vegetables, we were able to survive on these things.

One time during a ceasefire, my sister Amanie, my young brother Samir, who was only six, my other sister Ghada, and my cousin Wissam, were sitting out in the *dar* area of the house. Perhaps Amanie had a sixth sense, because suddenly, she urged her siblings to go inside. My two sisters and brother were just inside the door when an RPG grenade hit the stairs where they had been sitting. My aunt started to scream, thinking the children were still on the stairs. When a neighbour ran to the hospital and told me of the attack, I feared something terrible had happened and ran all the way home just to make sure that they were all still alive. With so many relatives living in that small house at one time, I was terrified that a single bomb would wipe out my entire family.

In spite of this hardship, life went on and women still had babies. I had done some midwifery nursing, so I knew a little about how to deliver a baby. But we also had *dayas*, or traditional midwives, who were very experienced. In the middle of one heavy bombardment, a woman came to the hospital and asked me to come and help her daughter-in-law, A'isha, who was in labour. Normally women would come to the hospital for delivery, but this woman was in too much pain and could not walk to the hospital, and the *daya* could not be reached. I hurried to A'isha's house and after examining her thought that she still had a few hours to go. I told her that it would be preferable if we could take her to the hospital when the fighting eased. Later, when it was quieter, I returned and with her relatives we carried her to the hospital where she had a lovely baby girl. This was the first delivery I'd done on my own and I was very happy and excited. When I told her waiting relatives and her husband, they were so happy and very relieved too. In the midst of all this horror and war there were still moments of joy and hope for us all.

◈◈◈

One day during a lull in the attacks, A'isha's mother-in-law invited us to come and have a cup of coffee with the family as a way of saying thank you for the safe delivery. We were very glad of the offer as by then coffee was a luxury. It was a period of quiet, but I came to hate these periods because people would come out of their houses thinking the attacks had ended and then, without warning, the shooting would start again, and many people would be wounded. The day we had the coffee was no exception. Just as we were savouring the warm black sweetness, heavy shelling erupted. We ran back to the hospital as the camp came under attack, and as we arrived, a family was brought in. In the respite from the siege and bombing, the Atoot family had been having breakfast in their *dar* when the first rocket of the barrage hit their house. One woman had shrapnel wounds; two of her children, aged six and seven, were killed immediately. A daughter had a wound in the femoral artery that spurted blood like a fountain and a son, aged five, had lost a leg and an arm. He was bleeding copiously and was still alive when he came to the hospital but died soon after. His sister also died. In one hit, the Atoot family lost nine people. During these repeated attacks on the camp, I had learned to suppress my emotional response and do what I could to save life. But the loss suffered by this family reflected my own personal fears and later, when I had a quiet moment, I was filled with overwhelming grief at this carnage and broke down and cried.

Throughout the siege, we nurses managed to carry out small operations, once, even saving a life with a cardiac injection—work not normally undertaken by nurses. When we undertook small operations to remove bullets and shrapnel, we had no anaesthetic or pain relief to offer. We would give the patient a wad of cloth to bite on. Sometimes I would joke with the patient saying, 'This won't be any worse than the pain of childbirth, so just bite on this and I will soon be done'. It was a cruel experience for the patient and us as well, but we had no choice.

Among the hundreds of wounded I remember, one boy stands out. He was about 10 years old, from the Snono family. He had a lovely round face with beautiful eyes and long eyelashes. His mother, who'd come with him, was beautiful too. He was wounded in the abdomen. Without an operating theatre or surgical instruments, or even a doctor to do surgery, there wasn't much I could do for him. I tried to settle him as best I could, but he was fully conscious and screaming in severe pain. He kept repeating, 'Why did they shoot me? I did nothing.'

It seems he got too close to the Amal fighters. There was no clearly marked border around the camp, and the distance between our houses and the Lebanese apartments was less than two metres. He told me he had looked at the fighters and gave them a 'thumbs up' sign. Then they shot him. He kept on saying, 'Why didn't they just swear back at me?'

He cried. I tried to calm him.

'I am still a child. I want to play, I don't want to die.'

After a few terrible hours he died, but I will never forget his words. This boy's face and these words and the manner of his killing and his agonising death, often come back to me in flashes of grief-filled memory.

◈◈◈

We had neither a morgue nor place to bury all the dead. Opposite Haifa Hospital there was a very small square for the unknown martyrs. Initially, we dug a big hole and buried all the bodies there. Then, as more people died, we had to find another place. We had to use some empty land in the camp just behind the clothing factory. It was a very dangerous spot, open and exposed. In normal circumstances in our culture we have our funerals at noon or in the afternoon, but now, for safety, people were buried at night or very early morning, with only two or three people from the family present. Even in death we were denied our dignity.

Throughout this time, we continued to try to contact the Red Cross, but they were still not permitted to enter the camp. A delegation from Iran was given access, though, to witness our plight. When they came through what could only be euphemistically described as a hospital, they were deeply moved by what they saw and the stories told by staff and survivors. They took lots of photos as well, and the next day, local and regional newspapers covered the story using many of these photos. But Nabih Berri, Amal's leader, accused the papers of using archival photos and even suggested they were from the Sabra and Shatila massacre.

Many Lebanese Shi'a were strongly opposed to this siege and attack on the camps, and during this time Hezbollah, which had openly opposed this violation against us, started to gain support among the Lebanese Shi'a population. After 10 days of fighting, a two-person delegation from the International Committee of the Red Cross did finally come to the camp and were allowed to take out critical cases. However, all the medicines they were bringing to us were confiscated before they were able to enter the camp. Then, as ambulances carrying the critically injured were leaving the camp, they were stopped by Amal militia and most of the patients were dragged out. Many of the people we sent out that day were never seen again. We believe they were killed, even though we never found their bodies. After that, the Red Cross again stayed away. I wept at this lack of humanity, this cruelty. Why was the world silent as we Palestinians suffered this brutality? As always, my despair soon turned to burning anger, and all my attempts at prayer during this time failed me.

However, my anger was tempered by the knowledge that not all Lebanese Shi'a were attacking us. Indeed, some risked their lives and the lives of their family members to help us. One Lebanese Shi'a family who lived close to one of the camp entrances was very supportive of the Palestinians. They did not let Amal take their building, and they told these fighters that they did not want any fighting in or around their building. Sometimes, this family would bring us medications and we used to send them money to buy us antibiotics and other drugs. But of course, they were afraid that they would be caught, and indeed, Amal did eventually kill their son, which meant they no longer dared to help us.

The siege dragged through the month of May into mid-June, with Amal unable to enter the camp or break our meagre defences, despite their superior weapons. Frustrated, one Friday, they eventually threatened us with total annihilation. Amal representatives told us on our walkie-talkie that fire engines stationed around the camp had been filled with petrol and that at midday, they intended to spray the whole camp with petrol and incinerate us, if we did not leave at once.

We could not believe what we had heard. I began to envisage people burning, dying a terrible death, panicking, terrified. People in the camp came running to the hospital, thinking they might be protected there. I fought to stay calm, but it was impossible. The thought of being burnt alive was too terrifying. There was a big debate among those people who had become the camp leaders during the siege and the ordinary people. Some thought we should surrender and let Amal fighters into the camp, arguing if we did not we would all be burned alive. Others, remembering the Tel al-Za'atar and the Sabra and Shatila massacre, felt that if we surrendered we would all be killed anyway. They felt that it was better to die fighting. Throughout that terrible morning, as this debate raged, one of the camp leaders got in touch with our people in Mar Elias camp and they started work to stop this horrific act. At prayers that Friday, an Imam from the small Kurdish community on the edge of the camp told his congregation what Amal was planning, and that such a crime must not be allowed to happen. He also contacted the other mosques in Beirut as well as all the Muslim religious leaders. After midday prayers, a large group of Lebanese and Kurdish Muslims who were living near the camp demonstrated in support of us. In the end we were saved from being massacred by the actions of these good people.

During the month-long siege more than 600 refugees had died in our camp alone, and more than 1500 had been wounded. In that same time, across all the camps in Lebanon, more than 2500 Palestinian refugees had been killed. In Burj Barajneh we had worked day and night; the hospital was filled to capacity with people in every room on beds and on mattresses on the floors. More than half of those who died did so because we could not evacuate them to receive proper treatment. We were in the middle of Beirut with all its facilities. Yet so many people, all refugees, women and children among them, died because we were under siege and were refused medical evacuation.

◈◈◈

I was 25 years old. My family had been refugees for 37 years. My people had been massacred in Dar Yesin and other towns and villages in Palestine by Jewish terrorists. Thousands had been massacred in the Lebanese camps of Tel al-Za'atar as well as in Sabra and Shatila by Christian Lebanese militia men. Now in Burj Barajneh, and other camps, yet another shocking war crime had been perpetrated against us, this time by people we considered our friends—Lebanese Muslims.

When the attacks on the camp stopped, the wounded were finally evacuated from the camp to other hospitals across Beirut. Doctors from these hospitals contacted Haifa Hospital and asked who had been caring for these people. They congratulated Walid and me and expressed surprise we had been able to stop femoral arterial bleeding for some eight patients whose lives had been saved by our actions. I explained what we had done: initially I put ice and very hard pressure on the wound with a tourniquet, and I told the family to release the tourniquet every 15 minutes, and then tighten it again. I would check the wound regularly, and if there was no more bleeding when we lifted the tourniquet, we assumed the wound had clotted. I explained to the families that the patient should have complete bed rest; and we gave them party balloons, to exercise their lungs as we didn't have any physiotherapists to give them the right breathing exercises. In some cases, we kept putting the tourniquet on their femoral artery for days and for one patient it was on and off for 10 days. But we saved their lives and their legs. Our doctors at the PRCS hospital at

Bar Ellias in the Beqaa told me when they asked the patients who had helped them they all said, 'Olfat'. It seems they thought of us as heroes. But God helped them really, because we did not do that much.

Our misery however did not end when the fighting stopped. The camp remained under siege with Amal militia forming a ring of military checkpoints around the camp at all entrances. People were starving, and the women needed desperately to get food for their families. On the day the attacks ended, women were allowed out of the camp to buy food. But they were told where to shop and forced to buy what the militiamen offered them. Then all the women, my mother included, were herded into one building and told to wait. They waited one hour and then another. By this time, they were convinced that at any moment they would be raped or killed. After four hours of this intimidation and fear, the women were allowed to return to the camp. When my mother came home, she threw the things she had been forced to buy in the bin, saying she would rather we all die from hunger than eat what she had bought. This intimidation and harassment went on for a full week after the military attacks were over.

That whole summer was tense. There was no fighting, but Amal remained dug in surrounding the camp. It was not easy for women to leave, and entirely forbidden for men. In fact the young men were not able to leave the camp confines for nine years as the siege was not lifted until 1994. As a result, many young men could not go to school. It was a virtual prison, one-kilometre square. Over time the young men in the camp became depressed, sleeping, smoking a lot and just being angry with their situation. They relied heavily on women to leave the camp for food and other essentials, but though frustrated at their confinement they were very appreciative of the work the women were doing. It was also a dangerous time for young women. Two nurses from the hospital were killed. The family of one of these nurses had a flat outside the camp and she went with another nurse to collect some valuables. Neighbours reported that when they were in the flat, they were both arrested. Ten days afterwards, their bodies were found outside Khaldeh. They had both been tortured before being killed.

In late June 1985, volunteer nurses from Norway came to the camp to work with us, and the Norwegian government donated some money to the PRCS to fit out an operating theatre and emergency room in Haifa Hospital. Our own doctors were now allowed back in the hospital, which with the new facilities, was a great relief and made us feel ready for whatever happened next. In August 1985, Helen came to discuss APHEDA projects with us, and as usual, stayed in our house. There were still a lot of clashes in and around Beirut so it was dangerous for her to travel. The camp was still surrounded by sandbags and checkpoints were everywhere. Things were very tense indeed. The night she arrived, the men were calling from the mosque loudspeaker system, warning us of the dangerous situation. We heard shelling on the edge of the camp and one person who was killed was carried past our house. We had absolutely no idea what would happen, but sleep was hard to come by that night as Amal started to shell around the camp.

The next day, Helen was supposed to go to Syria but stayed with us instead. We were glad of the moral support and incredibly grateful that people such as Helen and others from western countries could bear witness to our suffering and daily humiliations. We still had no electricity and no running water and every time we left and re-entered the camp through the Amal checkpoints, we suffered harassment and abuse. Helen was able to see, firsthand too, the destruction by Amal shells during the first siege, of the first APHEDA project, a children's day care centre to support working women. We had just started it, but afterwards we were able to fix the building and restart the project.

Not long after Helen left, in early September 1985 a second major attack with its associated siege and closure of the camp started. There was intense fighting as Amal tried every tactic to enter the camp. With the civil war in Lebanon raging no one could stop Amal.

There was no effective government. From outside Lebanon the PLO was lobbying to try and stop this fighting. Again, many people were injured and killed, but while we felt afraid and threatened, this time we were better prepared: with some small arms that had been smuggled into the camp. Lebanon was awash with arms so buying them was not difficult. The shelters were also cleaned so that people were better protected, and we now had an operating theatre in the hospital and both foreign and Palestinian surgeons as well as more nurses. Although we were in a much better situation, we still had no rest from this attack for 10 days.

◈◈◈

I continued to work at Haifa hospital and on the APHEDA projects until May 1986. But by then I knew I had to get away. I was so angry. I hated Beirut. I hated Lebanon. I just wanted to run away. I loved nursing, but I remember feeling I could not bear to see any more dead bodies or more blood or more wounded or more suffering. I constantly felt as though I was holding back a scream of overwhelming grief at all the loss of life I had witnessed. I was in a terrible dilemma. I was very attached to my family, my friends and my community but at the same time I had this urge to flee the horror that was our daily life. I was boiling with anger and humiliation and at the same time depressed. I was sleeping a lot, feeling very low and used to cry at night when my family could not see me. Around that time my brother Amer, then 18, decided to migrate to Sweden. I actually did not want to migrate, but I just wanted to get away. My other brother, Nader, had gone to the Gulf to work in order to support my family; and at that time it was relatively easy to get a short-term working visa in Dubai, especially as a registered nurse and a woman. So, Nader made the necessary visa arrangements and I prepared to leave.

On the day of my departure, I took a new pair of shoes with me to the airport, and just before I boarded the transit bus for the plane, I took off my old shoes, threw them in a garbage bin and put my new ones on. I did not want to carry so much as a grain of soil from Lebanon with me. The trauma of what I had seen and what I had experienced seemed to drive me to these extreme feelings, not just towards Lebanon, but towards the whole world. My life had been devoted to caring for people, but it had been full of blood, death and killings. I was at once overwhelmed by a sense of failure and despair, but also, with hatred and loathing. I can now understand what despair, desperation, and trauma can do to one's soul.

13

BAR ELIAS

I had hardly set foot in Dubai, before I regretted leaving Lebanon. Again it was events back home that caused this misgiving. After a few weeks, Amal imposed another siege on Burj Barajneh. This time, it lasted for 45 days. During the previous attacks, I had always been inside the camp and was aware of what was happening. But when I was away, I had no peace; I was glued to the television. This was worse in a way than living under the siege itself. I was in a constant state of heightened anxiety and apprehension.

Meanwhile, I tried desperately to adjust to a normal life in Dubai. I went to the Ministry of Health, did the nurses' registration exam and started work in the local hospital. But I could not stay. I could not work in this hospital, with all its facilities, electricity, water, food, sterile equipment, everything that in the camp my people were dying for lack of. I couldn't work when I had all this and knew my people had nothing.

Helen and I had done what we could to keep in touch over the months, so she knew I had gone to Dubai in April 1986. During this time she had made another project review visit to Beirut and had again experienced my people's situation for herself. Still in Dubai, I wrote to her after she returned to Australia about how depressed

and deeply traumatised I was feeling—I knew she would understand. She rang me as soon as she received my letter, very worried.
and suggested I see someone for treatment; and that it might be better for me to go somewhere closer to my family and friends. She advised me to go to the Syrian capital Damascus where I could be with
my old nursing and medical friends who had relocated from Beirut,
and where I could hear news of my family more easily. She also suggested it might be possible to work on the nurse training project that
APHEDA had established for refugees in Damascus and in the Beqaa Valley. My brother supported those suggestions as he could see
how depressed I had become. I had arrived in Dubai in May desperate to be free of the nightmare of life in Beirut, but the distance and
the comfort in Dubai had made it worse. In August 1986, after just
three months away, I went to Syria to again work with my people.

An old friend was waiting for me at the airport in Damascus. Initially I stayed with him and his family, which was not only a salve
to the soul, it was also practical. Unaccompanied, single women in
Syria faced many hurdles, chief among them finding accommodation in Damascus. In spite of these little difficulties, my depression
began to lift. I started sleeping properly; I was back working with
my people and had contact with people coming and going from Beirut to Damascus. As Helen had suggested, I was able to work with
the APHEDA projects in Damascus and the Beqaa Valley, using my
nurse training and community health experience I'd gained in the
UK and in Australia. I went to the Beqaa Valley on Fridays and Sat-
urdays and I worked in Damascus for the rest of the week.

On one of my first days in Damascus, I ran into Dr Mahmoud
Shehadi, a friend of mine, who was just about to return to Russia.
He asked if I had any messages for anyone that he should take back
with him. I answered, 'No, just say hello to friends there'. I had not
kept in touch with Mahmoud since we'd met last in 1982 in Bar
Elias, but of course I would think of him often, and knew from
his family that he was still in Russia. So, while I did not mention

Mahmoud by name, naturally I wanted Dr Shehadi to send him my greetings. And indeed, on his first day back in Kiev, Dr Shehadi saw Mahmoud and teasingly asked him, 'Guess who I saw yesterday in Damascus?' Mahmoud told me that he thought of me immediately. 'What is Olfat doing there? Where's she working?' he quizzed his friend, frustrated that Dr Shehadi did not know anything. But because it was difficult to be a single woman in Syria, he just assumed I had married and was working there.

Ten days later Mahmoud flew into Damascus. He was on his way to Beirut, but flying directly was difficult, so he came via Syria. By this time, he had been in Kiev for eight years studying and had graduated in cinematography with a master's degree.

Having found out from the student union in Damascus where I was staying, he knew I was not married, and rang immediately. It was around 10.30 at night; I was already in bed and my friend's daughter told me in the morning that he had rung and was in Damascus. At first, I thought she was mistaken and that it was Ahmed, his brother, who'd rung, but she told me it was definitely Mahmoud, just arrived from Russia, and that he wanted to see me. We met for coffee at the student union and caught up on all our news. We were both extremely happy to see each other. Neither of us was married, engaged or even in a relationship. We'd had no contact, but in my heart—even if I didn't know it—I had always loved Mahmoud. I was in love with him before and was in love with him still. My heart had always been engaged to him really and I was overjoyed to see him again. He was my dearest friend and I felt very happy when I was with him and I also felt safer and more secure. While my friends had been kind and generous I was still very lonely in Damscus.

Being with Mahmoud, who made me laugh and be more joyous, meant the loneliness lifted. I continued living with my friend's family, while Mahmoud stayed with students in the student union office. We were both anxious to get back to Beirut to our families, but it was difficult with the civil war raging. In time, of course, we came back to the old issue of marriage. We spent most of the next six months in each other's company but did not live together. I was working in the PRCS medical centre and in the hospital, and Mahmoud was working using his cinematography skills. We wanted to go back home so Mahmoud could talk to my family about our proposed marriage, but that was impossible, as by then the camp was in the grip of the fourth and longest siege by Amal—a siege that was to last six months. It was November 1986.

In normal circumstances, as was the custom, Mahmoud would have asked my father if we could marry. But because we could not contact him directly from Syria, we rang my brother in Dubai and he gave us his blessing on my father's behalf unreservedly. With the only impediment now removed, Mahmoud and I were married on 26 December 1986. Dressed in my blue jeans and a lovely peach-coloured blouse I had bought in Australia, we signed the Islamic marriage papers in the presence of the Sheik in Damascus, which meant we were married in religion. There was no formal family party, of course, although we did have a small gathering overseen by my friend, who acted as my guardian. Nor could our marriage be officially registered because neither of us had Syrian residency papers— our UN IDs were valid for Lebanon only. It was only when we returned to Lebanon several months later that we were able to register our marriage on April 1, 1987—so I have two anniversaries.

While still in Damascus, Mahmoud had found a job and my work for the APHEDA project gave me a small allowance, so we could afford to move into a small flat. We could also afford to buy our dinners to bring home. It was not only cheap, but essential, since I'd never learned to cook as a result of my mother's refusal to teach her daughters these things. When Mahmoud found out I couldn't cook he joked that he would give me one month to learn. Then he set about teaching me. Having lived away from his family and culture for so long, he had learned to cook out of necessity and was a patient and good teacher. As my mother predicted I learned kitchen craft quickly and since then I have made sure I spoil Mahmoud with my culinary expertise.

Even though we were desperately worried about our families, it was a happy time. We were together at last, and in love. In Damascus I had a short reprieve from all the horrors of war. We would spend hours at night talking about everything. He knew what had happened in the camps, but I told him all the details of the war and the siege. He was distressed, of course, as he had lost friends too. But he was very kind and gentle with me, and it was a healing time.

Early in January 1987, Helen came to Damascus again and, like all of us, found she could not enter Beirut by air, so she travelled overland by road instead. When she arrived, she was not allowed to enter the Burj Barajneh camp to review the various APHEDA projects, because it was still under siege. However, she was able to stay in Mar Elias camp in Beirut and review the projects as best she could from there. While in Beirut, she was able to speak by walkie-talkie to my father in the camp and to Mahmoud's brother, Ahmed, to let them know we were married. My father had been extremely worried about me being without family in Damascus and as he knew Mahmoud and liked him, he was very happy to hear this news, to know that I was safe and secure in my marriage. We both felt relieved our families knew for sure that we were married as I was soon pregnant. We were ecstatic to be having our first baby.

When the third Amal siege around the camps was lifted in early April 1987, I decided to take the risk and travel to Beirut to see my family. Mahmoud couldn't come with me as he had a film assignment. I could not bear to go to the camp alone, so I went first to his brother's house in Mar Elias camp and then with his mother to Burj. It had been 10 months since I'd seen my family and even though I was accustomed to our misery and poverty, I found it hard to believe what I saw. The camp had been bombed to rubble. More than 80 per cent of the houses had been destroyed and the rest had been badly damaged. No house in our area was undamaged. There was dust and rubble everywhere I looked. Some buildings were still smouldering and those still standing had been riddled by shrapnel blasts and bullets. All the water pipes had been damaged and water seeped through the alleys. The hunger and starvation in the camp was evident too. People were thin and gaunt. When I arrived at our house I was overwhelmed. All the family were pale and ill-looking. I held my mother and just sobbed uncontrollably. I simply couldn't contain my sorrow. The anger and hatred I'd felt when I departed Lebanon had dissipated, but I could not bear to witness their suffering. My poor family. What had they been through? My baby sister Ghada, and brother Samer, were like little sparrows, so thin. I hugged them to me, praying to make them better with my love. I could see they had been through a terrible time and a terrible war.

In time my mother and my relatives told me what they had experienced after I'd left. The camp residents had been expecting another siege. My mother was able to buy enough rice, sugar, onions, beans, canned fish and meat and other tinned food such as tomatoes and beans to store. But, of course, they could not store vegetables or meat. Because my mother was prepared, my family did not starve, but to this day my sister Hanadi can't bear lentils or canned beans because for months my family ate these daily. Many people also ran out of cooking gas, forcing them to use wooden doors and window frames as fuel. And, of course, there was no electricity and no light. My family had some candles for a while, but these soon ran out too; they had to make do with makeshift lamps that consisted of a small jar containing some fabric dipped in oil, as a wick. They could rarely go outside the house for a good six months. At first, they were able to hear the news on the radio but in time, the batteries ran out. Mostly they just sat and listened to the bombing.

Lack of water was a constant problem. During this siege, Amal shut off the water lines to the camp, but the heavy bombing exposed the aquifers under the camp, which meant people were able to gather the muddy water that collected in craters. The quality of this water was dubious, and predictably, many people became ill from drinking it. One time my mother was collecting water from such a place near our house. On her first trip she emptied the water into the containers in the house, then went back to collect more. On her way, she remembered she had left the water in the house uncovered so she went back to cover the water jars. At that moment, a shell hit the very place from where she had been collecting water—life and death was random.

Another time when the family was inside, three huge rockets hit our house. The two on the first floor caused a lot of damage and the third lodged unexploded between the wall of our house and the house next door, just near where the family was sitting. The instant the rockets hit, all the family ran terrified and screaming from the house. They were sure that at any second, the sitting room would be blown to pieces by the unexploded missile. Eventually, one of the young men in the camp, among the many now experienced in dealing with such ordnance, came and dismantled it. Although our house was badly damaged upstairs, my mother believes God was looking after all of my family during this siege. There were more than 25 people living in our house at the time, and nobody died. My little brother Samir, who was seven, lived in such perpetual terror that, according to my mother, he always slept with his hands on his ears and used to close his eyes tightly when there was bombing. Ghada, then 14, was so scared she would vomit whenever there was fighting. During this fourth siege, many people became so desperate for food they did things that were alien to our culture: slaughtering cats and dogs and horses for food. And, although it did not come to it, religious leaders had given people in the camp permission to eat human flesh. That was how shocking the situation was.

Whenever there was a ceasefire, women, desperate for food for their families, would try to break through the ring of armed men around the camp. This was very hard for them and all the family, but the men couldn't go as we knew they would be arrested, imprisoned or killed immediately. Sometimes the women would be let out, but when they tried to return with food snipers would often take pot-shots at them. More than 36 women were killed in this way while bringing food to their families. Men, including my father, waited at Haifa Hospital to assist their wives, inside the camp, out of sight of the snipers. There was talk, too, of some of these women being taken to a room outside the camp during this time and raped. Only God knows for sure. This is something we do not talk about.

My mother, like all the other mothers, suffered terribly. Aware of the huge risks involved, she tried to minimise her shopping trips by carrying huge quantities of shopping on her head. One day, needing flour for bread, our staple food, she carried a 50-kilogram bag of flour back to the camp via the airport road entrance. She told us afterwards: 'As I walked from the entrance of the camp to the hospital, I felt strange, dizzy, as if I was going to fall. It took me seven to 10 minutes and all the way I felt as if I had the weight of the world on my head and shoulders. I felt as if I would fall both from fatigue and from fear of being killed. When I met your father at the hospital and he took my load, I felt as if my joints had left me.'

Such journeys were often repeated as my mother struggled to feed the family. Later, she blamed her sickness, tiredness and severe arthritis as well as my father's diabetes, on the constant stress and fear of death and loss they lived with during all those dreadful years between 1982 and 1987.

By February 1987, Amal had begun to lose its ascendancy and the more Islamist-orientated Lebanese Shi'a movement, Hezbollah, had emerged. It had been actively resisting Israeli occupation since 1982 and by 1987 its military activities against Israel had accelerated. At the same time, in the absence of any effective government services in Lebanon, Hezbollah established a substantial network of clinics, hospitals, schools and social services together with a variety of small enterprises such as supermarkets that served the impoverished Lebanese Shi'a community. Many Shi'a had been opposed to the sieges and attacks on the camps, and some Amal fighters had defected to Hezbollah. It was also a time of anarchy and terror with foreigners the target of kidnappings and attacks. It was no surprise then that when an 8000-strong Syrian armed force was invited back into Beirut by the Lebanese Sunni Muslim Prime Minister, Rashid

Karami, to try to impose order, the Palestinians and others in West Beirut welcomed it.

With a ring of Syrian army checkpoints now around the camp, we started to feel more secure. However, Amal still maintained some checkpoints around the camp which meant our young men were still trapped inside.

14

NEW LIFE

I stayed in Beirut for a month before returning to Beqaa and Mahmoud in early May, where I continued to teach in the School of Nursing, planning to return to Beirut to have my baby with my family in September. When the time came, Mahmoud was away on a filming assignment. I did not have any pain, but I knew the baby was due and, in our culture, it is the custom to clean the house thoroughly before the baby arrives. I worked hard cleaning the flat and I was hoping to get to Beirut the next day before labour started. Around 3 a.m., I stopped cleaning and I slept until 5 a.m. I remember I had a beautiful dream where I was enjoying a walk in a huge garden filled to the brim with flowers. Even though I'd only slept for two hours, I felt joyous and rested when I woke. About 10 minutes after this, I had a colicky feeling in my stomach, but as it was Sunday morning I did not want to wake my neighbours. I was having a conversation with myself about what to do, when the pain started to become more severe. As I was not sure if this was normal, I decided to go next door and ask my neighbour. She explained my 'colicky feeling' was contractions and that I would have the baby that day.

I was so happy that the house was clean! I had a shower and, as I was drying my hair, the contractions started again. Each time I had a contraction I would throw the hairdryer on the bed until it was over; it took me more than an hour to dry my hair and put on my makeup. My neighbour came and asked me what I was thinking, explaining through her laughter, that the kohl, eye shadow and lipstick would be gone before the baby appeared.

Even though I had helped women in the camp deliver their babies and I knew about labour and delivery from my nursing studies, I was unsure of the pain I could expect with contractions and delivery. Having got myself ready I went to the hospital and, the minute I arrived, the contractions stopped. From fear, I am sure.

The doctor examined me and said he thought I would have the baby in the evening. He was a friend of Mahmoud's, having studied with him in Russia, and I was glad he was there with me. About half an hour later, I had such a severe contraction that I could not breathe. The doctor came back several hours later and was surprised I had not progressed with the birth in spite of all of these contractions.

Bar Elias is a small village in a rural area, and in such places it is a practice that older women, when they know a woman is in labour, go and pray by her bedside. These old women pray to Khadija, Fatima, A'isha and Zinab, and all the other Muslim holy women, to help the young woman as she delivers her child. On this day, several such old women came and sat by my bed, saying prayers from the Koran very loudly. While it was nice in a way, the manner in which they were praying made me think, 'Oh my God, I'm dying!'

Friends of mine—two female doctors who were there with me—very politely and nicely thanked these old ladies for their prayers and asked them to leave, as they could see I was very frightened. Then I started to bleed and as it was a very small hospital with no ultrasound, my doctor was worried the placenta might be starting to come away from the womb, and that I might need a caesarean. He asked me to stay in bed and be calm, but I was having terrible contractions every two minutes, and soon every minute, so it was pretty difficult to stay calm. However, between each contraction I would rest, and I would dream. They were pleasant dreams, and in one, I saw Mahmoud; and then I knew that I would be all right.

After many hours, because I was making no progress with the labour, the doctor called for the anaesthetist, but fortunately, surgery was averted when, at 2am, I was taken to the delivery room for a normal delivery. The nurses and doctors kept saying to me, 'It's okay, you can scream or cry out'. But I was actually very quiet, saying only, 'Oh my God, my God, my God'. After an 18-hour-long, very painful labour, our son, Chaker Khazaal, was born.

Afterwards, I was so completely and utterly exhausted, I just wanted to sleep. They put Chaker in my arms next to me, which was nice, but with a drip in one hand and Chaker in the other, I couldn't sleep. The doctor had left, and the nurses were busy, so I was alone: and it was the middle of the night. Of course, from the moment he was born Chaker wanted to talk all the time, and he was crying constantly. Then I wanted to cry, too. Fortunately, there was another woman in the room who had also just had a baby, and her mother was there and came to offer me help. I started to cry uncontrollably; I was feeling so alone at the time. This dear woman reassured me, by saying she would look after me as well as her daughter. She took Chaker then, and settled him, after which I was able to rest for a short while. When I woke up, I went to the toilet and promptly fainted. The nurses came running, of course, and put me back to bed. Then early that morning, supported by friends and neighbours, I was discharged. In all, I stayed only five hours in the hospital after the delivery. With Chaker wrapped up tightly, my neighbours took me back to my house and settled me in. In our faith have special prayers for newborn children and my neighbours recited these for Chaker. These prayers settled him and me as well.

My family was expecting me in Beirut, so when they heard the news, my sister, Amanie and Mahmoud's mother came the next day. We stayed for one week there and then went to Beirut by *service*, which at that time took around six hours. I was ready to go home. With winter approaching it was beginning to get very cold in the Beqaa. Besides, I really wanted to be with my family. In Beirut, my aunts, my grandmother, my mother and sisters all wanted to help me. It was good to be with them in spite of the dreadful circumstances of the camp. When my grandmother, Alia, came to congratulate me on Chaker's birth, she told me about her own deliveries.

'I was in the field when I had your uncle Ahmad,' she said. 'I started to have pain but I wanted to finish what I had started. I finished my work, went home and called my mother-in-law. "Why didn't you tell anyone?" She scolded me. I told her I had to finish my work. She told me to wash while she went for the midwife.

'We did not have a hospital then and so they put me on a chair with no seat. The midwife told me to push down hard. When I delivered, they caught the baby and cut the cord. By the next morning I was out in the field again. But my family fed me very well. My mother and my mother-in-law made all the food necessary for me to produce milk and to help my uterus contract. I drank lots of cinnamon tea with ginger and crushed mixed almonds, walnuts, pine nuts and pistachio because we believed this helped to contract the uterus. I also had a special drink made with cinnamon sticks, ginger, anise, cumin and coconut called ainar, which helped baby Ahmad and me expel gases and settle our stomachs. The coconut helped my milk to come.

'They made me omelettes with onions and lots of garlic and olive oil because we believed garlic also helps the uterus to contract and that eggs and oil would help me produce more milk. They would also make sweet dishes such as an omelette with sugar on top and also *Halaweh* made from sesame and sugar, and other flavourings because we believed these things are also excellent for producing milk. At the same time there were foods that I could only eat in small amounts such as cucumber and *mulukhiya,* a green vegetable high in iron, generally cooked with beef or lamb or chicken rich in protein. *Mulukhiya* causes loose bowels and we believed the baby would have diarrhoea if we ate too much of this when I was breastfeeding.'

Alia also told me how she took her children with her when she went to the field every morning. She would make a swing for the babies and let the older children play in the fields. The babies were wrapped up and secured in the small swing and given a special dummy made by the women. This dummy, called *lahive*, consisted of a clean piece of material wrapped around a small piece of home-made Turkish delight and a mixture of ground herbs such as anise, cinnamon, almonds and crystal sugar. The children would love to suck this dummy. Alia told me she never had difficulties with her children as they were happy playing in the fields out in the open air.

I would hear these stories of her life in Palestine and share with her the joyous memory but also feel cheated that my children would not feel the grass of Palestine beneath their feet and instead their playground was a squalid camp stalked by death and terror.

Still sometimes camp life produced moments that were like a shaft of light in the darkness. Just after I returned to Beirut with Chaker, I developed a terrible toothache. It was early October 1987 around 6 p.m. There was then still a curfew at night, which meant no one was allowed to leave or enter the camp after 7 p.m. But with the pain becoming acute I desperately needed to see a dentist. As there were no dentists in the camp, I went to a checkpoint and asked the Syrians if I could leave, knowing there was no way I could possibly return within the hour. I didn't care about the danger as I was in a pain so excruciating that it felt as if my face would explode. The problem was I was still breastfeeding Chaker so, of course, I could not stay out all night until the curfew was lifted in the morning. I had Chaker's birth certificate with me as evidence of his recent birth, and the Syrians were sympathetic and promised to help me.

But Amal had a second ring of checkpoints around the camp that I had to get past. They were not so helpful, insisting I go to their headquarters for permission. I knew if I did so, I would be longer than an hour; and there was no guarantee I would be given permission anyway. I silently said a prayer and decided to go straight to the dentist, a Lebanese Shi'a, and deal with the fallout later. My heart sank when I walked into his waiting room—it was full; I was the eleventh or twelfth patient at least. All I could think of was, 'Oh my God, I will be here until 10 o'clock'.

When the dentist came out, he told all those waiting that I had an appointment. I looked at him and said he was mistaken. But he insisted. Once inside his surgery, he said, 'I know you are Palestinian from the camp, and I know about the curfew. You cannot wait here.' He was so kind. He stopped the pain, put in a temporary filling and asked me to return in the morning. I was back in the camp by 7 p.m. thanks to this wonderful man.

I stayed in Beirut with Chaker for three months, until December 1987, when Mahmoud returned from his filming assignment, and we could both go back to the Beqaa Valley. Life there was simple and people were pleasant and helpful. I resumed working in the School of Nursing, leaving Chaker with the neighbours the hours I was teaching because it did not have a childcare centre. Once, when it snowed heavily and Mahmoud was away, I became a bit frightened of being alone in the house with Chaker. The neighbours invited me over and I spent the night with them. I have good memories of my time there because of people like these. In fact, this is the kind of hospitality cultures like ours were famous for before the endless wars that have wreaked the Middle East.

While there, I used to visit my parents and other relatives in Beirut from time to time, but then Mahmoud started to work in Beirut and he was only able to come back to the Beqaa on weekends. So, with mixed feelings, we decided to move to Beirut around October 1988. We had been in the Beqaa for 18 months and it had been the happiest of times.

I was, of course, still teaching nursing students. The training project was very successful, and we graduated a number of nurses for the PRCS hospitals in Lebanon. I worked with our people in Wavell camp in Balbek, as well as with those Palestinians who lived in the local community throughout the Beqaa. We provided welfare services, and monitored pregnant women and newborn children, assisting them with clothes and other necessities. Through this community-based work, I gained a lot of knowledge about monitoring and managing projects funded by overseas agencies, and I learned

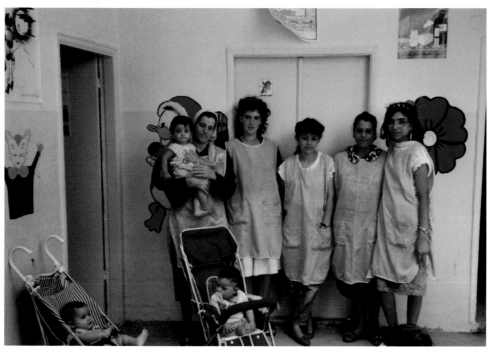

The first nursery, set up by Olfat in Burj Barajneh camp, 1988.

Olfat (third from right) with childcare workers in one of the Union Aid Abroad APHEDA-funded childcare centres in Burj Barajneh camp (managed by Olfat), 1991.

Olfat with colleagues outside the Women's Humanitarian Early Education Centre and Nursery Centre, supported by APHEDA through AusAid. Burj Barajneh refugee camp, Beirut, 1996.

View over Burj Barajneh Palestinian refugee camp in 2001.

Olfat in an alleyway of the Burj Barajneh Palestinian refugee camp where she lived until recently. Water and electricity lines intermingle overhead, at times causing deaths from electrocution. Beirut, 2010.

Olfat with other international students on a peace-making course at the Kofi Annan Peace Center in Accra, Ghana, 2009.

Olfat and Helen with Union Aid Abroad Staff APHEDA, L-R Ken Davis, Helen McCue (APHEDA co-founder), Melissa Park MP, Olfat, Jeremy Smith. Parliament House, Canberra, Australia, 2014.

Olfat with Marie Bashir, Governor
of New South Wales, Sydney, 1996.

Olfat with Ged Kearney, then President of the
ACTU and Chair of APHEDA. Sydney, 2014.

Olfat at the United Nations where she spoke on the plight of Palestinian refugees in Lebanon,
New York, 2015.

Olfat at the United Nations with UN Secretary General Ban Ki-moon. New York 2015.

Olfat speaking at a Union Aid Abroad APHEDA fund-raising dinner.
Wollongong, Australia, 2014.

View of Tarshiha and surrounds, 2016.

Photos of Olfat's son, now a Canadian citizen and as a result, the first member of the family allowed to visit Tarshiha. At right, with an elderly Arab resident. Tarshiha, 2016.

Olfat with her son Chaker after her address at the UN. New York, 2015.

about the financial management and reporting requirements necessary for such projects. Most importantly for me was the practical and immediate help we were able to provide for our people right there in the community, which helped to make their lives a bit better than it would otherwise have been.

By April 1988, many PLO soldiers had returned to the camps to protect us after Arafat negotiated an end to the camp wars with the Amal militia leadership the year before. However much to my dismay this did not bring an end to the wars. Fighting in the camps re-ignited, this time between two PLO factions in Beirut, causing loss of life and yet more pain and suffering for the residents. I believed our focus was to liberate Palestine and to fight the Israeli occupation, not ourselves.

Through this time, we had some news of our people in Palestine but no real contact. Not since my visit to England had I met anyone who lived in Palestine. What news we heard was via radio or TV. Email was not yet available and phone contact impossible. We did, of course, hear of the December 1987 Intifada, or uprising, in the West Bank and Gaza Strip. Like Palestinians everywhere, we supported our people inside the Occupied Territories who had risen up after 20 years of oppressive Israeli occupation, of land seizures and extensive construction of Israeli settlements on their land. I was proud of the role that women played in this uprising, helping with first-aid and relief work, and setting up makeshift schools so their children's education could continue. I often thought of the friends I had met in London and prayed for their safety especially as young people of my age were confronting the powerful Israeli army with stones alone.

In Lebanon, sectarian fighting had continued sporadically throughout 1987 and 1988 and the Lebanese Shi'a were actively engaging the Israelis in the south. By 1989, Lebanon effectively had two governments, one led by a Christian President, General Michel Aoun, based in East Beirut and the other led by Selim al Hoss, a Sunni Muslim Prime Minister, based in West Beirut. Amal and Hezbollah had been fighting for control of the southern suburbs of

Beirut, and the Syrians had control over most of the central business district and all of the Beqaa Valley. In October 1989, attempts at reconciliation between the fighting factions by Arab states, in particular Saudi Arabia, led to the signing of the Ta'if Accords.[23] These detailed a process of constitutional change that would lead to democratic and representative elections. Lebanon, it seemed, was finally on the road to recovery.

◇◇◇

When Mahmoud, Chaker and I returned to the camp in October 1988, we had no alternative but to live with my parents and my siblings, as there was no place in the camp for us to rent and very few buildings that didn't need serious repair work. Nor could Mahmoud and I afford to build another storey on my parents' place. This meant that there were 10 of us living in the tiny house. After six months, we were eventually able to get a small flat in the Fakhanie area, near the Arab University. Of course, like most of the buildings, this flat, had been damaged during the war – it took us more than two months to fix it sufficiently for us to live in it. We had brought all our furniture from the Beqaa and, with difficulty, our little family settled into the flat in March 1989. Chaker was 18 months old and by then I was pregnant with our second child. In spite of our difficulties in the camp, it was a peaceful and joyous time in my life.

During these years we saw Helen regularly for 10 days or two weeks at a time, every six months or so. She would travel to southern Africa and then Palestine to review APHEDA projects there, and then come and see us in Lebanon. In February 1989, she undertook a one-month teaching assignment with Lebanese community health nurses for the World Health Organisation. Her work was right on the Green Line, previously a line of trees and vegetation that divided East Beirut from West Beirut at the Museum Crossing in

---

23 The Ta'if Agreement negotiated in Ta'if, Saudi Arabia and signed on October 22, 1989, was an agreement to end the decades-long Lebanese Civil War, reassert Lebanese authority in Southern Lebanon (then occupied by Israel), and set a timeframe for Syrian withdrawal.

central Beirut. She stayed with us during this time, which we really enjoyed—when you are living such a confined life, it is refreshing to have an outsider bringing news and views from places of order and freedom.

After the 1982 invasion, there had been few international development agencies in Beirut, since the region was considered unsafe for foreigners. There were even fewer agencies working with Palestinians. To their great credit, the Norwegian non-government agencies had stayed, and were supporting a number of our projects, but this was thinly spread. So APHEDA's support to us through all those difficult years was greatly appreciated. I had two part-time jobs that were both funded by APHEDA: a childcare project at Mar Elias camp in Beirut, and my teaching in the School of Nursing at Bar Elias. Two days a week I would travel to Beqaa Valley for this, leaving Chaker with my sister Amanie.

We had just settled into our flat when on March 18, 1989, when another of Lebanon's wars started. This time Aoun was fighting the left-wing Lebanese forces as well as the Syrians, who were dug in around the UNESCO area and the Sports City in downtown Beirut. Our flat was on the eighth floor of a building right between these two areas. The height of the building in Beirut at the time was always a problem, not just because of the lack of electricity, but because tall buildings always got hit when the bombing and shooting started. We were friendly with a Syrian family from Damascus on the fourth floor, so when there was fighting, we would stay with them. As the fighting continued, they (wisely) decided to return to Syria, leaving us the key to the flat and inviting us to use it any time, which we did.

Now as a mother and wife, the situation put me in a dilemma. I was very fearful for Chaker but at the same time I did not want to leave Mahmoud alone in the flat. At that time there were no armed Palestinians in Beirut and there was no fighting around the camp, so we felt that it was safer inside the camp. Eventually we agreed that Chaker should go and stay with my family in Burj, though. We hoped he wouldn't be too distressed as he had lived there before and he was used to my parents, brothers, sisters and cousins. I would go to the camp and see him every day after work and then come back to the flat. I was working in Mar Elias camp near our flat and would travel by *service* to Burj Barajneh and back to Fakhanie to the flat. Normally this journey would take 10 minutes or so but at that time, it could sometimes take 90 minutes because there were so many checkpoints and the traffic was congested. I did that for two months, from March until early May, but it was dangerous and stressful in this war situation. Also, by then I was nearly two months' pregnant with Fayez. Poor Fayez, right from the beginning his life was filled with fear and violence.

One day in the middle of this war there was a ceasefire. All was quiet. Teenagers from the flats were playing soccer on a playground nearby. Mahmoud and I were watching them from our balcony. Eventually, becoming bored I decided to go inside and read. I left Mahmoud on the balcony and lay down with a book. Sometime later, I was taking a break from reading and was looking towards the mountains when I saw a bright flash. I wanted to scream, but the scream stayed in my throat. I knew instantly it was a rocket, and I thought it had hit the balcony. I could not hear a thing. There was smoke everywhere. I cried out to Mahmoud and rushed out to see if he was still alive. Mahmoud thought the bedroom had been hit because of the smoke, and he was crying out as he came in to find me. Then it dawned on us—the rocket had hit the playground. We felt sick with fear for all the children and spectators. When the dust settled we ran to the balcony to see what we imagined would be carnage below. But by some miracle the rocket had hit a neighbouring empty soccer field and not the playground.

Mahmoud looked at me and said, 'Don't be afraid, my dear. Just sit down.'

I was surprised. He added, 'You are fine. Nothing is wrong with you, just sit down.' Then I saw that I was bleeding. I had on a long loose cotton dress and I was bleeding from my stomach. There was a lot of blood. I did not have any pain, but there were small cuts on my stomach and on my legs made by small shards of glass. I went to the hospital nearby, but my injuries were only superficial. Poor Fayez, though. More shocks for him—before he had even been born.

Returning from the hospital, a few hours later, I went to lie down but noticed the pillow where I had been lying before the blast was hot. Then I saw that a large piece of shrapnel had cut through the pillow and had driven deep into the mattress, missing my head by millimetres. I kept that pillow for a long time—if it had hit my head I would have been killed instantly; and I thanked God I had lived. There has never been any doubt in my mind that I will leave this world only when God wants me to. That day, and other events in my life, just confirmed this profoundly. That day my time had not yet arrived.

After this experience, Mahmoud and I agreed we should leave the flat and return to the family home in the camp despite it already being very crowded; now there were seven family members plus the three of us, in a tiny space. Of course, it was difficult to have any semblance of a married life, so we tried several more times to repair the flat and live in it. Twice we repaired it and twice it was shelled in various clashes. Then the war flared up again in earnest and again, the flat was shelled; this time many of our things were destroyed. The bombing was much heavier this time and many people were killed on the streets. I couldn't even leave the house to go to work. On this occasion, the camp was not under attack because it was Lebanese Christians who were fighting each other and also fighting the Syrians.

By now I was around six months' pregnant with Fayez. We went back to my parents' house around July 1989 and stayed there. On December 25, our second boy was born. In contrast to my first pregnancy, this time I gave birth within the bosom of all my family. A long ceasefire was holding; we hoped this meant the war was finally over. A month after Fayez was born we repaired the flat yet again and with my sister Ghada to help me and the children, we returned to live there. My mother begged me to stay in the camp, but I insisted we were leaving. The day after we moved out, the Lebanese President Renae Mowad was assassinated, so fighting broke out again and we returned to my parents' house.

More than ever we needed a place of our own. Mahmoud's brother, who had recently migrated to Sweden, offered his place above my mother-in-law's small house in the camp, which we accepted with alacrity. Finally, we had a place of our own near all of my family. It was a huge relief. Of course, that house, too, had been damaged during the war and needed to be repaired, but we felt secure back in our community. Throughout this whole time of war and repairing places to live, and having babies, I was also working full-time managing the APHEDA-supported childcare centre in Mar Elias and another centre we had established in Burj Barajneh. My skills in project management were improving and increasingly I started to move away from nursing to work more in the community, focusing on the needs of women and children in our camps. I was well-known in all the camps in Beirut and in our community in the Beqaa, and I was beginning to develop my skills in community leadership. Mahmoud and my family, especially my father, were most supportive of my work, and Helen encouraged me as well. I felt the voice I had found in Australia in 1984 was re-emerging after years of trauma and war.

My two children went to the Burj Barajneh centre, which was close to my parents' house. So if I were delayed, my father would collect the children and take them home—no doubt telling them all the stories he used to entertain us with, especially those about his life in Tarshiha. We had also started a small maternity shop and a cooperative where women could buy baby clothes, nappies, milk powder, toys and such things, as they needed. I continued to go Bar Elias to teach, but as there were now other teachers there, I was only going once a week, since it was a long and tiring day: I used to leave the house at 6 a.m. for a 9 o'clock start, then would leave at 3 o'clock to be back in the camp by 7 p.m. At that time, we had to go the long way through the Druze-held areas of the mountainous areas of the

Shouf. The three-hour trip each way by *service* was exhausting, but the highway from Beirut to Damascus was still controlled by the Christian Lebanese Forces so there was no way we could risk that. In fact, that route was closed to us for 15 years, from 1975 until 1990.

Life in the camp was still difficult, even to undertake the simplest tasks. For instance, we needed permission from the Syrians, who at that time controlled the camp perimeter, to bring our furniture into the new house. And the actual process of moving was laborious, mostly because we could not bring our car into the camp, since all the entrances were blocked. Mahmoud had a small car he used for his media work, but the closest he could get it to our house was the checkpoint on Airport Boulevard which was about a a five-minute walk from our house through the narrow lanes of the camp.

By the middle of 1990, we all thought the civil war in Lebanon was over but, towards the end of that year, the tensions between the Christian factions in East Beirut and the Syrians that had been simmering for more than a year, erupted again. The day this happened, I was packing lunch for the children and preparing to go to work. Fayez was less than a year old. I was holding him, and Chaker was standing next to me when I heard military aircraft overhead. Then the heavy bombing started. I screamed, and of course, the children started to scream too. Grabbing both of them in my arms, I ran to Mahmoud, who was resting in the bedroom, and shouted, 'They are shooting and bombing the camp'. I ran downstairs to Mahmoud's mother. The fear I felt was unlike anything I had felt on previous attacks; it was an overwhelming fear for my children. As it rose inside me, to the point of hysteria, I crushed them to me, terrified they would be harmed. Our house was on the border of the camp, which left us exposed to any fighting. Above us the Syrian air force and Lebanese planes of General Aoun were fighting each other. In the meantime, my father had rushed to our house and helped take the children to my family's house in the middle of the camp. As we ran, the planes passed right overhead tailing and shooting at each other. I was screaming. The children were screaming. All of us hysterical with fear.

Racing towards my parents' house, my mind went back to my childhood years and the anger I would feel when I had to endure yet another humiliation at the hands of soldiers at a military checkpoint. I used to come home and take my anger out on my grandmother and say, 'Why did you leave Palestine. This is all your fault! It would have been better if you had stayed and died there than this life we have.' My grandmother would take my anger and explain softly that they had fled to keep their children safe. It was that day, as I raced with my father, Chaker and Fayez, that I understood her at last. Like her I would have gone anywhere in that moment to keep my babies safe. So, when we arrived at our home, I walked up to my grandmother and simply said, 'sorry'.

After several days of heavy fighting, on October 13, 1990 Aoun agreed to a ceasefire. He eventually left Lebanon for exile in France. That was the end of 15 years of bloody civil war in Lebanon. East and West Beirut opened up, and soon after parliamentary elections were held. We all celebrated, of course. People went to see the Green Line that had divided the city for 15 long, bloody and senseless years. There had been so much destruction and so many deaths. And for what purpose? It was a question none of us could answer.

15

THE PROMISE OF OSLO

Finally, peace bought freedom to travel throughout the country. We took advantage of this new-found liberty to visit the Beqaa and our friends and relatives in the south. Our journeys showed us a country disfigured by individual and collective scars. It was also a country still occupied by the Israelis in the south; and the Syrian army remained the major military force keeping the peace. And sadly, our place as Palestinian refugees in Lebanon, remained as tenuous as ever. We were still denied the right to Lebanese citizenship but could not return to our homes that were now part of Israel. So, we remained stateless, without passports, and denied basic civic rights such as the right to work or access to state-run health and education. We could of course go to private hospitals, universities and schools, but very few camp residents had the money to afford this. The UN through UNRWA provided medical services and education, but these were basic and in the case of schooling ended before the last year of high school. Sadly, this remains the status quo even today.

Back then our lives, and the lives of most Lebanese people, continued to be dogged by material hardship. We faced multiple obstacles daily. We had only two or three hours of electricity a day and sometimes we would go for days without any at all. In the summer we could not store food, as it would perish, so I had to go shopping every day. We also had major water shortages. Inevitably I would be halfway through a machine-load of washing when the electricity would go off. On going to bed at night I would leave the bedroom light switch on so that when the electricity came on in the middle of the night I could wake up to do the washing. With two young boys, I needed to wash regularly. The ironing was done with a heavy old metal iron that I heated on the gas stove.

Sometimes we would go to have a shower only to find the water was off because the electric pump that brought the underground water we use for washing only, into the roof tank, would have stopped. Even after all these years, our drinking water still came from the camp water point which we would carry to the house in a one-gallon can, that I kept under the kitchen sink. Often, I would go to get a drink only to find the can empty. So, off I would have to go to the water point and carry the heavy cans back to the house and up the stairs. UNRWA collected the rubbish and waste from the camp, but right near our house was a rubbish tip, which the rats loved. It was always smelly and a major health hazard. While I, like the majority of Palestinian women, worked hard to keep our homes and children spotless, are surroundings were appalling. One of the biggest dangers was the network of electricity wires that hung low over the narrow laneways and homes like a spiderweb. Dangling wires and water seeping from the broken and cracked pipes were a lethal combination and could mean sudden and unexpected death.

Stuck in these miserable, unhealthy, unhygienic and poverty-ridden refugee camps, it was hard not to feel bitter about our daily struggle. Especially as we knew life in our home town of Tarshiha would not have been like this. This bitterness, anger, constant tension and fear took a great toll on the physical and psychological health of the people in camp.

During this time, my mother's arthritis became much worse, aggravated by her anxiety over my brother, Abu Khalil. In 1989 amid the siege, he had left the camps to try and catch a ferry to Cyprus. In undertaking this perilous journey, he'd been helped by Christian friends, but was captured by the Christian militia, the Phalange. When we heard this news, we were sure he would be killed. I spent six months searching for him, praying by some miracle he had been spared; going from place to place, looking for people we knew who had contact with the Phalange, trying to find out what had happened. My mother became extremely ill and depressed.

By a strange twist of fate, a good turn my brother had rendered to a captured Phalangist in the early days of the civil war was repaid. This person, seeing my brother in prison and remembering his own rescue, in turned saved my brother. After six months, Abu Khalil was released and left for Cyprus, to live with my uncle there. My mother had been greatly relieved when she heard he was safe in Cyprus. But, unable to find work, my brother took up an offer of a job in Baghdad. The day after he arrived in August 1990, the first Gulf War started; and we had no news of him for another six months. My mother's depression returned; she was always in tears, seeking comfort in prayers for her son's safety. Her mobility, diminished by her swollen and painful joints, became so much worse, as if all the years of grief had accumulated in her body, making her ill.

Not a single refugee family in the Middle East was unaffected by the Gulf War, and the situation in the camps became even more precarious. As a result of Arafat's support for Iraq, some 350,000 Palestinian refugees were ordered out of Kuwait and other Gulf States, where they had been working on temporary work visas, many for several decades. Those who had left Lebanon as refugees had to return as there was nowhere else for them to go. But in the post-civil war situation, there were few jobs and even fewer places to live. In addition, hundreds of families had relied entirely on the financial remittances of their relatives working in the Gulf, among them were my Uncle Bashir and his family who had to return to Beirut, and my Aunt Khadija and her family, who had to go back to Allepo in Syria. Dependent families were plunged deeper into poverty.

In 1992 our third son, Hadi, arrived—another fourth-genera-tion Palestinian refugee, born in a country that wanted him gone. Our hopes of fulfilling Lebanon's wish to see us leave, were further dashed in 1993, in what I, and many refugees in the camps, saw as a betrayal by our own people. In the early 1990s secret discussions had begun between the PLO and members of Israel's 'peace camp', which eventually led to the Madrid Conference, convened in Octo-ber 1991. These talks centred on UN Security Resolutions 242 and 338, which dealt with the results of the Arab-Israeli wars of 1967 and 1973 as well as the issue of the Right of Return of all Palestin-ian refugees. But there were major differences in interpretation. Is-rael saw these resolutions as referring only to the 1967 'displaced', while the Palestinians understood them to refer to both the 1967 and 1948 refugees. We were pleased when Palestine's chief negotia-tor Haider Abdul-Shafi, and others at the conference acknowledged there would be no lasting peace without a resolution of the refugee situation.

But during this conference PLO Chairman Yasser Arafat, with-out consulting key players in his delegation, undertook secret dis-cussions, hosted by Norway, with the Israelis. The result of these discussions became known as the Oslo Accords.[24] So, on September 9, 1993, Arafat and Israeli President Yitzhak Rabin signed letters of mutual recognition and later in an historic moment shook hands on the lawns of the US White House, with President Bill Clinton looking on. In these documents the PLO accepted, as it had done earlier, that the state of Israel had the right to live in peace and se-curity. This written assurance gave Israel its long-sought recognition of legitimacy. But these letters did not mention the Palestinian right to self-determination nor the Right of Return of all Palestinian refu-gees. Those letters, signed by both parties, addressed the refugees of 1967 only, leaving the issue of the 1948 refugees, the majority of us in Lebanon, for the so-called 'final status' talks.

---

24 Friedman, Thomas, 'Rabin and Arafat seal their accord', *New York Times*, September 13, 1993.

In reaching this agreement, both parties chose to ignore the UN General Assembly Resolution 194 (1948), which explicitly states the right (as granted to all refugees under international law) of Palestinians to return to their homeland. Needless to say, Palestinian refugees in Lebanon, and throughout the Middle East, saw the Oslo Accords as an outright betrayal by our leaders. We were devastated.[25]

In Burj Barajneh, as in all the other camps in Lebanon, the residents, even Arafat supporters, were furious. What had all our sacrifice been about? Why had so many of our people died in the struggle for the liberation of Palestine, for our right to return home, only to be ignored at a critical moment? Our future looked bleak indeed. Many people were saying in disgust and anger, 'They have eaten our meat and thrown our bones to the dogs'. We saw clearly what our leaders had done. We knew why Israel was happy. The Oslo Accords allowed Israel to keep 73 per cent of the land, to be responsible for 97 per cent of the security, and to control 80 per cent of the water of the West Bank and Gaza Strip. But though our leaders betrayed us, we knew this agreement would not work because the key element—justice for the Palestinian people—had not been addressed. We knew, too, that eventually our people in Palestine, hundreds of thousands of refugees like us, would resist this agreement and fight again for our rights. When Palestinians, and our supporters among the Lebanese, demonstrated against the Oslo Accords in the streets of Beirut later in 1993, the Lebanese army attacked the demonstrators, killing 40 people and wounding many others.

Soon after the signing of the accords, Arafat and his supporters were allowed to return to Gaza where the Palestinians began working to develop a new constitution and a democratically elected Palestinian National Authority (PNA). When the elections for the PNA were held, some five million Palestinians in exile and in refugee camps throughout the Middle East were not permitted to vote.

25 Aruri, N, 2001, *Towards Convening a congress of return and self-determination, Palestinian Refugees: The Right of Return*, Pluto Press, p. 260.

Only Palestinians in Gaza and the West Bank could exercise this democratic right. Again, we felt abandoned and were furious.

The Oslo Accords also directly affected economic and social life in the camps. Until then we had had support from UNRWA, the PLO and, increasingly, support from the international community through non-government aid organisations. But, afterwards much of this support dwindled with the international aid community shifting its financial resources to the West Bank and Gaza. UNRWA cut back its much-needed services, the PLO greatly reduced its support to welfare services, and the response from the governments of Australia and Norway was much the same. We had to struggle to keep our projects afloat.

We had become the forgotten people of Palestine.

During this time Helen and APHEDA remained staunch supporters of our projects and helped to keep the issue of the 1948 Palestinian refugees in the news. In 1992, Helen convinced the then Australian Foreign Minister, Gareth Evans, to visit the camps—the first government minister from any country to visit the camps since 1948. I imagine it must have been quite a shock for Mr Evans to see first-hand the alleyways and war-ravaged buildings; and a nightmare for his security to allow him to wander through our streets and houses. The visit was an extraordinary moment for camp residents and is still remembered today. At that time, Lebanon was a mess. No Arab politicians had ever visited us, and even officials from the Palestinian Authority would come to Beirut and not enter the camps. When Mr Evans walked along our laneways people just couldn't believe he was there—it was an amazing morale boost for us and gave Australia an abiding place in our hearts.

◈ ◈ ◈

In the wake of the Oslo agreement, I realised the Palestinian refugees in Lebanon would have to now rely more on our own resources. I decided that, as women, we had to do what we could for ourselves—we could not rely on our political leadership. I wanted to start to work more effectively with the international community, too, and knew that I had to seek their support if we were ever to return to our homeland. By then I had been working with my community in Burj Barajneh for 18 years. I was well known and respected, and had a position of leadership within the camp. My initial focus was the creation of employment opportunities for the many women who were widowed or caring for physically or mentally disabled/war-damaged husbands or sons. In 1993, to address these concerns a group of us established the Palestinian Women's Humanitarian Organisation (PWHO)—the management board consisting of highly regarded women representatives of the local community.

Through my connections with Helen, I contacted APHEDA and with its help we were able to develop this organisation and get some important projects off the ground, including job training in the new information technology industry, and in more traditional areas, such as dressmaking and hairdressing. We also initiated much-needed childcare projects, after-school tutoring and summer school programs for children, and importantly for me, we aimed to keep our culture alive through a program that taught our young about Palestine and customs such as our traditional dance, *Debkeh*. We also sought to empower women in the camps with workshops on their rights under Islamic law, and health and literacy education that gave them insights into how they could obey religious laws but still have planned pregnancies.

Critically we also sought to look after our elderly – knowing the Lebanese Government would not. From my own family experience I saw how hard it was for my grandparents to remain mobile and healthy after so many years of deprivation and war. I felt we owed it to our elders to do whatever we could to make them comfortable. Using my community nursing experiences in Australia, our organisation trained nurses in home care — delivering the treatment our aged residents required to their door.

We also developed our own skills and became adept at lobbying international agencies for their support – within a few years we had projects sponsored by NGOs such as UNIPAL in the UK, PAL-COM in Norway, and volunteers working in our camps from Canada, Australia and Scandinavia. These connections gave us valuable links with which to educate people in the wider world about our lives, as these mostly young volunteers went back to their countries and talked about what they had seen and experienced, raising their voices in support of our rights as refugees.

Over the years my work with the Palestinian Women's Health Organisation has defined me and remains one of my proudest achievements. It was the launch pad for my work internationally as an advocate for my people and gave me the platform on which to take our story into the world. The fact that we have been able to keep the organisation running through funding cuts, war and threats from extremists belies how important it is to civil society within the camp, and for me it has been the source of great friendships and support.

As if I didn't have enough on my plate at this time, I began a sociology degree at the Arabic University in Beirut that year as well. We didn't have much of a social life in the camps—we couldn't go to movies or restaurants—so at night, we would often just sit in front of the television. At the time, Mahmoud was working nights, so I thought I should benefit from my free time rather than waste it. Although I did have a young family, I had a lot of help from my sisters and parents, so I knew I could juggle everything. That did not stop me feeling nervous at the idea, as I had never been to university and had not studied since 1984. I was also conscious of my age, but the younger students were very welcoming and helpful. I studied sociology, psychology and philosophy and found it a great opportunity to explore Arab and Islamic philosophy. That first degree was the start of a love affair with academic life.

My ongoing relationship and friendship with Helen brought me to Australia many times. In March 1996 I came as a guest of Union Aid Abroad-APHEDA. It was a timely invitation as the Australian Government was now directing its aid to the Occupied Territories, and PWHO's financial situation was precarious. I travelled across

Australia holding meetings every day. It was a month of solid work, but it was a valuable opportunity to speak publicly about our plight and raise much-needed funds. But there were some difficult moments. I recall meeting officers from AusAid, the Australian government agency responsible for overseas aid, whose decisions made the difference between whether or not a woman in our camp could feed her children. Yet they had no idea about our situation. I made sure that was rectified and I like to think I had some impact as we secured ongoing government aid for our work. But it certainly brought home to me the importance of face-to-face contact with donors.

◈◈◈

Back in Lebanon, facing increasing Hezbollah-led Shi'a resistance to their occupation of the south of the country, in April 1996 the Israelis launched yet another massive ground assault in southern Lebanon, bombing Haret Hreik, a Shi'a area bordering Burj Barajneh camp, and attacking Hezbollah offices, causing extensive damage. These offices were in a high-density civilian inner suburb of Beirut so this attack killed many Lebanese civilians and wounded more in the flats close by. Nearly 500,000 people, Palestinian and Lebanese, were displaced from south Lebanon; and, of course, many came for shelter and support to Haret Hreik. These people stayed for a month until the attack in the south abated. PWHO and many of the camp children, including my own, worked day and night to get mattresses and blankets and food for them, with the support of some international aid agencies.

Unperturbed by the 1996 Israeli invasion, the Lebanese Hezbollah fighters intensified resistance to the occupation of their land. In 1998, the Israelis bombed Beirut relentlessly. One attack—on June 24—was particularly frightening. When it started in the late evening, bombs fell so near the camp that the children woke screaming. We all raced to my sister-in-law's place, which was more sheltered than our place. Chaker, as always, was loudly expressing his anxiety, but Fayez was quiet, just sitting with his eyes wide open, seemingly numb. Andrea, a Canadian volunteer who was staying with us at that time, was understandably terrified. The bombing sounded very close to the camp. As we huddled together, we talked about Israel's intention to destroy Lebanon's infrastructure. During a lull in the bombing, Fayez turned to me and quietly asked, 'Mum, what is infrastructure?' I explained it was things such as electricity, water, roads and bridges, and that Israel was bombing these in retaliation for the Hezbollah's attempts to liberate occupied southern Lebanon. With a big sigh of relief, he said, 'Thank God, we do not have any infrastructure in the camp. It means they won't bomb us tonight, doesn't it?' Amid fear and tears there was laughter.

At that moment, I also thought of my grandparents and parents and everything they had lost. Instead of growing old in their homeland with the beautiful mountains in the distance and fresh air, sustained by food from their own farm, they suffered with chronic and painful illnesses brought on by the miserable damp, crowded, existence in the camps and the lack of proper health facilities.

16

LIFE AND DEATH

My father had always worked and supported the family well, but during the civil war he became unemployed. Eventually he was able to get a job as an accountant with SAMED, a manufacturing enterprise run by the PLO in our camp. However, the factory was destroyed in 1985 during the Amal siege. With the PLO infrastructure largely dismantled after the 1982 Israeli invasion, and with no funds available for repairs, the factory workers and the 350 families they supported in Burj Barajneh camp faced a difficult time. My brother in the Gulf and all of us, supported my parents financially, but it was still not easy for my father to be unemployed and unable to support his family. He did, however, work with the popular committee, representing the Tarshiha people. This made him well known and respected within the camp, and of course it boosted his morale; but it was still hard for him not to be able to contribute to the family finances.

Over the years my father had developed diabetes, which had become common in the camp. During our various wars and sieges, with all the stresses they imposed, it was not easy to manage his condition, although he was monitored by the UNRWA clinic since the mid-1980s. We all believed his illness resulted, not from poor diet so much from daily stress. My mother, too, suffered from a worsening arthritic condition which caused her considerable pain and eventually serious disability. As a family, we did our best to support our parents, and not a day would pass when I would not see either of them. When they were well they were a great help with the children, and my boys spent a lot of time with them in my family home and greatly loved them both.

In 1997, I became pregnant with our fourth child. Mahmoud and I had always wanted a baby girl and the boys, too, were keen to have a sister. By late January 1998, I was in my eighth month of the pregnancy. As it is normally very cold then, it is not really a good time for spring-cleaning, but I wanted to get the house ready for the baby. As usual I was a bit obsessive about cleaning. It could have waited, but no, I wanted it done. One night after I had finished, I felt very ill and started to vomit. I began to lose my balance and had a severe headache. I called my sister-in-law, Nakeyah, who put my feet in cold water and prayed over me, which seemed to make me feel a bit better.

Early next morning, Helen rang from Australia and said she'd had a feeling I was not well. I reassured her I was fine and sent the children to school as usual, before going off to the doctor with my friend, Suhair. I was shocked to find that my blood pressure was sky high—200 over 110. I was immediately admitted to Makassed General Hospital in the city, with a condition called pre-eclampsia which, if untreated, can kill both mother and baby. Helen, who had been planning to visit, brought her trip forward when she heard how ill I was, and was at my bedside within two days, staying with us for the next two months.

Over the next few days, my blood pressure came down slowly, but not by very much. The doctors decided to induce the baby and for 24 hours I had contractions every two minutes. I was in so much pain and absolutely exhausted. Finally, the doctors decided I should have a caesarean despite my blood pressure being still dangerously high. We were all very frightened—I was very scared that I would die. Mahmoud came with me to the reception section of the operating theatre; he was very supportive, but we were both crying. When they took me into the operating theatre I became even more terrified when the anaesthetist, obviously thinking that I could not understand English, said to the surgeon, 'Why did you call me? I can't I give her an anaesthetic with such high blood pressure. Did you bring me here to kill her?'

My doctor then spoke to me in English, explaining the various procedures and attempting to calm me. 'We will give you an epidural but we cannot give you any sedation to go with this,' she said. 'So, while you will not feel pain, you will feel the sensations. Normally we give a sedative but as your blood pressure is high I cannot give you one. So be strong and as soon as the baby is delivered we will give you some sedation.'

Then began the worst experience of my life. I was absolutely terrified. When they cut my abdomen, there was no pain, but I could feel the sensation of the retractors they used to pull the abdominal wall open to get the baby out. As they pulled, I cried out, 'It feels like an earthquake in my tummy. Something is going thump, thump, thump in my tummy!'

When all my other babies had been delivered normally I never cried out. Now, even with the epidural I was hysterical. The doctor, who was gentle and kind, said, 'Take it easy, my dear, take it easy. When we take the baby out we will make you comfortable'.

Finally, when I heard the baby cry I, too, cried with happiness and relief. Hani had been born. Immediately after I was sedated. It was 13 February 1998. I was moved to the intensive care unit where I remained for the 10 long and difficult days that it took for my blood pressure to come down. Hani was in the nursery, having been born three weeks' premature. When I first saw him I nearly fainted as he was so tiny and covered by too many tubes. The day I left the hospital, he could not come with me, which left me very miserable. The whole episode had been a terrible and terrifying time for all the family, but we later joked that I must still have something to do on earth;

the angel of death had come visiting again, but we asked him to go away one more time.

As Hani and I gained our strength, everyone fussed over our little survivor. As is our custom after a birth, we slaughtered two sheep. I really dislike this practice as I am a vegetarian, but it is a custom that is widely practised. We distributed meat to the poor people in the camp and barbecued enough for the family celebration. We also made *karawaria*, a special dish made by all families after a baby is born: a mixture of rice flour, caraway flour and water. This mixture is stirred all through the cooking process so as not to go lumpy, and is served cooled in small plates, with a variety of nuts, mainly pistachio and walnuts, and coconut sprinkled on top. Traditionally, the sweet is given to everyone who comes to visit—which in this case, felt like half the camp! Helen, who stayed on to help me in my convalescence, became an expert at making this sweet.

Eventually I was strong enough to return to work and we continued to develop our programs within the Palestinian Women's Humanitarian Organisation. By 1999, PWHO's contacts with international aid agencies and support groups had increased considerably. The Norwegian group PALCOM, which had been sending volunteers to the camp since the mid-1990s, invited me to Norway that year to speak about our situation to non-government agencies, the government aid agency, universities and church support groups. I travelled all over Norway and saw how proud people seemed to be about the country's role in the Oslo Accords. This was not surprising, given that their government had acted as a midwife to the deal. They were all under the illusion these Accords would help solve the Palestinian problem. But when I told them of our situation post-1993 and showed them how the Oslo Accords had done nothing for us, many people were surprised. They were quite unaware the agreement sought to deprive us of our right to return to Palestine, as guaranteed by international law and by the many UN resolutions passed on the issue. I see our role in making people aware about the situation of the 1948 refugees, as one of the most important things that we Palestinians can do.

As in Australia, there were moments of frustration, especially with government officials. I often felt, when talking with them, that our projects were the victims of international aid fashion trends, whereas for us, they were a matter of survival. For instance, one year we would be told the focus was on income-generating projects, which of course we supported. But the next year the focus was on women, which we also supported, though really we wanted both income-generation and a better life for women. Often when we tried to determine our development priorities in a given year, we would learn that the international focus might be on something else. I feel that government agencies need to understand our material situation.

Regardless of these frustrations, I was glad to seize the opportunity to visit Norway and, alongside my work in raising awareness, I was able to secure funds for our aged-care program from an organisation called Focus working through PALCOM. PWHO also developed a relationship with a nursing school in Norway that ran a program of overseas work experience and sent students to us for experience with our aged-care program.

Soon after my return from Norway in 1999, I began to have trouble with my voice. Numerous tests and scans revealed thyroid cancer. Fortunately, with radiotherapy and respite in a Catholic convent in Damascus where the nuns cared for me wonderfully, I went into remission. But I found the necessary separation from the children and family very difficult. Again, I thought that death had come searching for me and still, it seemed it was not yet my time. All these near-misses in my personal life increased my faith in God but also made me realise I was still alive for a reason and that my work for my people had not yet ended.

In September 2000, our people were again provoked when then Israeli Opposition Leader, Ariel Sharon—despised by Palestinians for his role in the Shatila massacre—and a Likud delegation, protected by riot police, provocatively entered the Temple Mount complex in the Old City of Jerusalem, which houses the Al-Aqsa (Dome of the Rock) mosque—the third holiest site in Islam.[26] The al-Aqsa Intifada inside Palestine started soon after this incident, and another bloody chapter in our fight for our rights began.

By then, without progress on the peace front and with the occupation becoming more brutal and settlements construction escalating, support for Hamas had spread throughout the Occupied Territories. In Lebanon, political change has been obvious too. I observed the posters and wall slogans supporting the nationalist parties: the PLO or PFLP or DFLP, had given way to posters and slogans that were more religious in tone. As people's hopes of a return to Palestine were dashed over and over again, many lost hope in the political process and turned to religion, both Islam and Christianity. But among our people only a few turned to extremism. Among Muslim women, as an outward expression of their faith, many started to wear the hijab, or scarf, and more conservative codes of dress. The slogans and posters on the wall now referred to Jerusalem as the capital of Palestine and to our other Islamic holy places. Lebanese-based Palestinians, banned for many years from undertaking the Hajj due to the troubles in Lebanon, were finally given permission by the Saudi Government to make the religious pilgrimage to the holy cities of Mecca and Medina. People now felt only God could solve their problems.

As my family was more secular than religious, these pilgrimages did not hold any interest for us—and by then my parents were to ill to travel anyway. By the late 1990s, my father's health had begun to deteriorate. After Hani was born in 1998, my father developed a serious wound on his foot that due to his diabetes quickly turned gangrenous. We did everything we could to try to save his leg, but eventually, in May 1998 it was amputated. He had difficulty adjusting to this as there were few rehabilitation facilities and no physiotherapy in the camp. We tried to get him to use an artificial leg but it was too

---

26   Goldberg, S. 'Rioting as Sharon visits Islam holy site', *The Guardian*, September 29, 2000. https://www.theguardian.com/world/2000/sep/29/israel

hard. Getting around in the camp either on crutches or in a wheel-chair was impossible in the small alleyways filled with obstacles.

During the later years of his illness he was mostly confined to a small room upstairs in our family house. Still he continued to be a member of the Tarshiha committee helping all people, whether in the camp or overseas, to maintain links with the village's community. In addition, he wrote down all his recollections of his life, his family, his community and the history he had lived through.

A year after his first amputation, he bumped his other foot and again the toes became gangrenous. At first he refused to have any-thing done. By this time my father just wanted to die. Eventually he consented to having the toes removed, but of course this did not help, and ultimately, he had to have the second leg amputated above the knee. It was a terrible time for he and my mother, as by now quite crippled by her arthritis, she found it difficult to care for him.

Our family was scattered around the world and during this time we felt deeply the pain of our separation from each other, laid on top as it was, of our exile from Palestine. My parents missed their children greatly. Nader was in Dubai, Amer was in Sweden, Ha-nadi and Amernie had married and were in the US with their hus-bands and children, and my aunts were in Syria, Cyprus or Germany. Samir was still at school.

My father was very special to me. He taught me to be strong and independent and he treated me as an equal to my brothers. This was so different from the experience of many of my female friends from more traditional families. He was a wonderful role model, teaching me to love, not hate. He taught me to think for myself. Even as a teenager he gave me freedom to live my life as I wanted to, all while helping me develop an ethical and moral framework to make the right decisions in life. This framework remains with me and helps me live my life today.

As I watched his health failing I remembered the good times we had spent together—how we would play, eat and pray together as a family, and he would tell us, *'Palestine ma daa't ma bedea'. Hak wara mtaleb'*—so long as we keep struggling, our right to return to Palestine will not be lost.

My father was the rock of the family whom I loved dearly; so, to see him suffering was extremely heartbreaking. Eventually, as his health deteriorated further, and he lay dying, his mind wandered. He was not always aware of us, or of who we were. At this time, he talked about Palestine and Tarshiha, his village, not as though he were remembering it, but as though he was really there. He told us he was picking figs, catching birds, and he was talking to friends who had died before him. He was walking about his farm, enjoying being there, almost as if the past 54 years had not happened.

Despite being grief-stricken I was happy for him. His last days were spent back in his homeland, in his village. And no one could stop him—no soldiers, no checkpoint could prevent his soul's journey back to his beloved Tarshiha.

◇ ◇ ◇

My father's death was the beginning of an ending. Six months later, on November 10, 2002, my mother died. Now only my grandmother remained as the family's last physical link with Tarshiha. Our parents had been born in Tarshiha, we were the camp children who had been raised on memories. My mother's death, however, crystallised for me my role as a spokesperson for my people. I had been meant to travel to Australia on November 11, but when my mother fell ill I postponed the trip. The day my mother died I slept in and missed her last moments; maybe subconsciously, I didn't want to see her die. Although I was full of grief, my family urged me to go to Australia. My aunt told me how proud my mother was of my work overseas and my role as the voice of our people. I came to see her death as a message; she died so I would go. I boarded the plane just hours after her funeral and cried all the way across the Indian Ocean to Sydney.

17

WOMAN ON A MISSION

In the years after my parents' death, my commitment to serve my homeland and my people deepened. I felt a desperate need to keep hope alive within our community and to keep the path towards peace open. It made for an interesting marriage and family life as I began to travel more frequently, speaking at international events and being sponsored to undertake training to further the work of our NGO.

In the first decade of the new millennium I told my people's story too many times to count, travelling to Australia seven times and Sweden five times; speaking at conferences in Paris, Cairo and at pro-Palestinian rallies in Austria, the UK, Norway, Sri Lanka and wherever I was invited. At the same time, I participated in workshops and courses on the plight of refugees, gender-based violence and women's issues; but always my travels were inspired by the desire to have our voice heard in the world.

It was during a 2004 visit to Australia that my family's last living link with our homeland was lost. My grandmother was 95 years old and in great health—but her life had in many ways stopped when she left Tarshiha; her stories were always of the time before the camps. When I was having children, she would talk to me about her own experiences in giving birth. But she only ever spoke of those babies born in Palestine as if by denying her life in the camp she could deny history. On my second night in Sydney, I was lying awake in the early hours of the morning when I saw my grandmother at the end of my bed smiling at me. I immediately rang my family back in Lebanon, but when Chaker answered, he assured me my grandmother was fine. I went back to bed and slept. In the morning, Chaker rang to say just moments after I had hung up, he had received a call from his uncle to say grandmother had died. Although the news saddened me, I felt at peace knowing she had travelled to be with me to say one last goodbye.

My place and reputation among my community was disrupted in January 2006 when a group of men moved into the camp near the cemetery. Our security measurements were very weak, and we had no idea who they were. The following month, as a woman-led NGO, we began to experience attacks from different parties who were spreading rumours about us. We were accused of trying to convert children to Christianity and encouraging women to divorce. Our community was being told not to use our services.

When an article appeared in an extremist newspaper about us, I went to see the popular committee chairperson and demanded a meeting with my accusers. When I arrived with two of my staff members at the meeting there were around 15 men waiting there. They started accusing us of giving children alcohol and allowing them to have sex when they went camping as part of our summer program. I was outraged, asking them where the evidence was for these claims. They told me I would have to shut the organisation down. I refused, saying, 'Who are you to ask us to close down?'

After another two days they called me back again and said, 'We are not here to ask your opinion, Olfat. We are here to tell you what you will do.'

And again, I said, 'Who are you to tell me what to do!'

These accusations and threats went on for four months, during which time they sent me personally threatening letters and distributed leaflets in the camp making scurrilous claims about our group and our work. It became quite dangerous especially because I continued to defy them. At one stage, I was threatened with, 'We will not kill you, instead we will let you cry all your life'. I saw that as a threat against my family, so for a month I stopped going to work; and was so terrified for the safety of my children that I wouldn't let my children out of my sight.

In a bid to fight back, one day, a group of PWHO employees including myself, held a silent protest outside the mosque to coincide with Friday prayers. I spoke directly with the men as they arrived.

'You know my family very well. You know how active we are in the Palestinian cause. You know that during the war I stayed in the hospital working day and night for a whole month. I could have stayed home with my family, but I didn't.' I reminded them of all the things we did for them.

Then they started saying, 'Yes, yes she is right, we remember when she did this,' and 'Yes she's a good woman. She didn't leave us.'

But the threats continued. By the end of a month at home I realised my actions were helping them win, so I decided to see the sheikh at the only mosque in the camp. I said to him, 'I want to know how this problem started. We have been working here for so many years; I have been through all the wars here. If I am a bad person, why have I stayed here and supported my community.'

The sheikh admitted he should not have believed the accusations and instead, should have investigated more. In the end, the dispute was solved, and everyone was quite embarrassed by how they had treated us and by the way they were so easily misled by rumour. Later, I found out the group of men who had recently moved into the camp and had started the rumours were Sunni Islamic extremists. They had been trying to recruit young refugee men, so had tried to divide our community and create instability to help their own cause. The easiest way to do that was to attack civil society and the programs and structures that made us a community. The PWHO was an easy target because we were not backed by a political party. Also, as a high-profile woman who does not wear the hijab, I would have been a threat to them.

The men left as suddenly as they arrived, and the camp was just settling back into a normal routine when our world was, again, turned upside down. In response to the capture of two Israeli soldiers by Hezbollah, during July and August of 2006, Israel launched its heaviest bombardment of Lebanon in 24 years. While we were not the targets of the attacks, we were caught in the middle. By then I was living outside Burj Barajneh camp, in a nearby suburb. When the attack began, we all assumed it would be over in two or three days. But then the airport was closed, and the rockets continued. As soon as the war started, people rushed to the supermarkets for supplies, and within hours the shops were empty. Immediately, I began to think how I could help my people in the camp and provide them with prompt assistance. On July 15, I visited the camp, searching for answers to my question. Despite the danger, people were determined to stay, saying, 'We are already refugees. Do we need to be refugees again?'

Three days later when I went back to the camp, I was horrified by the devastation. My car was the only moving vehicle. Every place was in deep silence, destroyed—all the buildings and roads were totally smashed. It felt like a ghost town. I was overwhelmed. The smell of death and destruction was everywhere. People were amazed when they saw me arrive: 'How did you come,' they all were asking. We held a meeting of all the NGOs in the camp and, again, people insisted they would not leave the camp, despite the threat they were under. Their reasoning was: 'We became refugees once, so we are not leaving. If we will die, we will die.' So, they stayed, and they watched and experienced every minute of that terrible devastating 33-day war.

The PWHO had a summer activity program ready to go, but the attacks meant it was no longer feasible. I contacted APHEDA in Australia who were funding the camps and asked if I could use the money for relief work instead. They agreed, and also began a fund-raising campaign back in Australia to support us. While Israel made it clear the camps were not a target, Hezbollah, which was located in the surrounding areas, was. I began to visit the camp daily, delivering emergency food and hygiene parcels to help residents survive. The camp was isolated because Israeli planes were targeting any vehicles that drove out along the airport road. I decided to take my car and leave the worry about my life in God's hands—when my time is over, it will be over, no amount of hiding in safe places will help.

Helen was very concerned about my activities and rang me from Australia to plead with me to be careful: 'Olfat you know the Israeli drones are always flying overhead. They'll notice you coming and going every day and will put a question mark on your car. You could be targeted.'

If I hadn't been worried before her call, I was now. But we still needed to get supplies to the camp. PWHO staff member and Lebanese physiotherapist, Amal Shammas, and Hiba Izdahmad, who worked with PWHO and had curly, long thick red hair, used to come with me each day. During one of our daily trips to the camp, I remembered Helen's warning and said to Hiba, 'Quick, put your head out of the car!' When she queried my strange request, I repeated, 'Please put your head out the car, and Amal, rest your arm out the car. I'll explain later.'

When we got to the camp they demanded an explanation and I said, 'So Israelis see your hair is not covered, Hiba, so you are not Hezbollah; and your arm is not covered, Amal, so you are not either'. We kept doing this for the 33 days, driving with our heads and our arms out the car windows.

18

MY PERSONAL DIASPORA

In 2006, I also had to face a fact I had long been dreading—the beginning of my own diaspora. Chaker, who had always done well in his studies, having won a scholarship to go to a private high school in Beirut, was determined to leave and study abroad. This became possible when he won a scholarship to York University in Toronto and moved to Canada, where he has since acquired citizenship. All Palestinians face this problem—my mother had a big family, but by the time she died, they were scattered to the four corners of the world. It is not easy as a mother to have your first child leave home and live in a foreign country, even Canada, but at the same time I was realistic: what would he do if he stayed here with his family?

Like any parent, I wanted a good and secure future for him, which, for Palestinians, often means trying to move overseas, because in Lebanon there are many professions that Palestinians are not allowed to pursue for various historical and administrative reasons. For instance, you can't be a doctor, engineer, banker or even a taxi driver. Mahmoud and our family were fortunate because he was working in the media which was allowed. The consequence of these restrictions is that most children are no longer motivated to complete their education, so few young people have the opportunity to study abroad. When Chaker told me he was leaving, I could understand, but it didn't make it any easier.

Looking to my own future and still in love with academia after completing my Bachelor degree in 1997, I continued my studies in psychology, with a focus on women. In 2010, I was awarded a master's degree and in September 2016, I finally became the doctor I had first dreamed of being as a teenager, when I was granted a PhD in Psychology from the Beirut Arab University. I am the first in my family to gain a PhD and as I accepted my doctorate I could feel the presence of my parents and grandparents—I know they would have been so proud of my academic achievements as I continued to live out their belief that education rather than war, would free our people.[27]

During these years I continued as Director of PWHO but was also able to work as a casual lecturer in Women's Studies at the Arab University – as academia was not on the list of jobs denied to Palestinians in Lebanon. While our family is well off compared with many other refugees, life remains challenging: regular cuts in electricity makes managing the household and ensuring my boys continue their studies a struggle. In the camp, one of more urgent concerns is the state of residents' homes. The camp buildings are old and substantially damaged by all the conflict, so are dangerous for residents, often collapsing; in the winter, the streets are flooded. Last year, while in my office in the camp, a large piece of the roof fell on top of me, and I was very lucky not be have been seriously injured. Rebuilding or repairing has been made more difficult since May 2010, when Lebanese security forces banned the bringing of building materials into the camp.

As the population grows and people expand their homes upward, there is no natural light, no insulation from the winter storms or the heat in the summer. At times it feels like we have made no movement forward since the first refugees arrived. And should we begin

---

27 Only 1% of the world's refugee population has a bachelor's degree.

to feel at home, there is always another law to remind us we are not welcome. In 2009, the Lebanese government passed an amendment to an earlier Lebanese Nationality Law excluding even those children born to a Palestinian father and a Lebanese mother from the right to nationality, ostensibly to prevent resettlement of refugees.

The work of PWHO continues but has been affected by regional events such as the war in Iraq and Syria, making funding for our ongoing projects more precarious than usual. Our long-term allies, such as Union Aid Abroad-APHEDA from Australia, continue to support us, but their grants have diminished with the aid demands of the regional conflicts. When I had come under attack in the camps by the Islamist groups, Helen was insisting it was time I emigrated to Australia. It was a temptation. I knew my family and I would have a good life there and could still campaign for my people. But I couldn't leave. I believed then, and still feel, it is my duty to serve my country, to be a voice when others can't speak—this is the one way I can serve my people.

During the Israeli bombing raids of July 2006, I spent a lot of time speaking with media outside—I was interviewed by PBS in America, my letters detailing the situation were appearing on social media sites, and media organisations would ring me for the latest news on what was happening in the camp and to the people there. Whenever I am asked to speak I always say yes, because I want to make sure the world does not turn away. I am like the conscience of the international community—I will not let them forget. I am angry with Israel, but I am angrier with the world community. In 1947, the whole world decided on dividing Palestine into two states; and they have to be held responsible for that decision and the many others that have let Israel prosper at our expense.

For example, in 1949 the international community allowed Israel to take its seat at the UN, ignoring that an original requirement for its membership was that Israel fulfilled the Right of Return accorded to Palestinian refugees in UN Resolution 194, passed in 1948. If Israel had been forced to implement Resolution 194 before it took its seat on the UN, the Palestinian refugee problem would not exist today, and descendants of the 1948 exiles, who have inherited their parents' refugee status, would instead, have inherited the citizenship accorded to their parents in historic Palestine. This is why we are suffering.

Sometimes my anger with our situation is hard to contain, especially as it affects us individually. In 2009, I was invited to Sri Lanka, but looked likely to miss the event because I could not secure a visa. When I visited the embassy to know why there was a delay, I soon realised they were concerned I would try to remain in Sri Lanka. I could not stop myself, 'Because I am a refugee you are frightened to give me a visa? Look at my UNRWA refugee travel documents and see where I have been—Australia, Norway, the UK. They all gave me visas, and you will not?' The officer was very embarrassed and immediately stamped my papers.

In 2012, I was again faced by a similar humiliation. I was flying with Qatar airlines to Nairobi for a course on gender-based violence. The plane was late, so we missed our connection in Doha and were provided with an overnight stay before the next flight was due to leave. I had already missed a night's sleep as our first flight was at 3 a.m. so I was exhausted. The airline offered vouchers for accommodation. One by one passengers were called forward and directed to their hotel. However, when my name had not been called, I asked an airline official what was happening, and was told that I could not leave the airport as I had no passport and was a refugee.

It felt as though a lifetime's anger suddenly erupted inside me. 'Where am I meant to stay the night?' I asked. 'At the airport? I am a woman. I need my privacy! Would you accept this if I was your mother, or your wife?' He replied that I was not allowed to enter the country. Again, I burst out, 'Who are you to allow me or not allow me? It's not your country that rejects me, I reject your country.' And with that, leaving some very confused staff in my wake, I demanded they get me a flight out of Qatar. So, I found myself flying back to Jordan and then on to Nairobi. By the time I landed in Jordan I was laughing about the incident, but it just emphasised to me yet again the ultimate betrayal of a world community that created our problem in the first place yet is happy to wipe its hands of our situation.

My tours and speeches around the world culminated in June 2015 when I was invited to represent Lebanon's Palestinian refugees at a ceremony marking the formation of UNRWA, with UN Secretary-General Ban Ki-moon in New York. It was an incredible honour to be there on the world stage and I carried the spirit of my parents with me, knowing how incredibly proud they would have been to see me there. I wanted to make the audience understand the reality of our life by asking them to re-imagine their world.

It's the 21st century and we are here in New York. Try to imagine an area of about one square kilometre in this city—the size of some of the camps in Lebanon—into which 37,000 people are squeezed. That is a population density 50 per cent greater than Manhattan, which has the highest population density in the whole of the US. This one square kilometre has limited clean water, electricity installations that are unreliable and unsafe; a maze of alleyways that are so narrow only one person can walk down them; and a sewage system that cannot meet the needs of the population.

This is the 21st-century experience of Palestinian refugees. For us the phrase 'human rights', and the right to be 'free from statelessness' have all lost their meaning.

Of course, people always ask, 'What do you think the solution is?' I say, 'It's the right of return'. That is the only solution. I didn't choose to be a refugee. I didn't choose to come to Lebanon. My grandparents did not come to Lebanon to live; they came for what they thought would be a few weeks until things settled down in Palestine. It was not their decision to leave Palestine—they were forced away at gunpoint. I was born to refugee parents. I am still a refugee and my children are refugees. But I believe we will return. I have not given up hope, but I like to say my hopes are frozen. The day we lose our hope, that will be the real *al Nakba*; that will be our real catastrophe.

My words received a great response, but of course, nothing has changed. And while my hopes may be frozen, unfortunately my life is not. I grow old and my children have grown up. Like any mother I have immense pride in the adults my children have become; and despite the horrendous experiences of their lives, they are generous and tolerant human beings. Chaker has taken his place in the world: he has worked out of Dubai in a not-for-profit company giving refugees remote employment in areas such as e-marketing, social media and web development. In 2016, Arabian Business Magazine named him as the most important Arab aged under 40. He is an advocate for refugees and aspiring young writers, and has published two books: *Confessions of a War Child* and *Tale of Tala*—both books being about the lives of refugees. I often reflect that his success flows back to my mother's insistence that I put my studies first: it would be through education that we could win back our homeland, but it is also education that has given us a path out of the poverty of the camps.

Thanks to Hadi and Fayez, Mahmoud and I finally have the daughters we craved as they both became engaged in 2017. Sadly though, they live away. Fayez, who has completed his accountancy studies lives in Bahrain and works in auditing, and Hadi is in Kiev where he is studying for his master's in communication. Hani, my youngest, remains in Lebanon and is completing his degree in communications.

I worry for their future as Palestinians—after 70 years Palestinians are still locked out of jobs and their rights in Lebanese society are still minimal. The collapse of Syria and the ongoing conflicts in the region have added to our precarious position. Thousands of Palestinians in Syria have fled to family in the Lebanese camps, straining the already meagre resources we have. The camps are now old—they were never built to be permanent; hundreds of homes are barely fit for habitation and are on the brink of collapse. PWHO has worked with this latest influx of refugees, providing language classes in English and Arabic as well as skills training for women. The rise of the Islamic State in Iraq and Syria (ISIS) and other extremists has also given me cause for great concern. Should their power grow in Lebanon that will be the time when I will finally leave. I want to be close to my culture, but I will not live under the control of fundamentalists like ISIS.

I am now 58 and still I am stateless. In 1984, my grandparents' house in Burj Barajneh was bombed and completely flattened. Among the precious items lost that day was the key to their house in Tarshiha. It was never found, but to keep our memory of their home alive, we had another key cut. In 1948, when Israel's first Prime Minister, David Ben-Gurion, was asked how he would deal with the Palestinians whose lands were confiscated and had been deported, he reportedly said, 'The old will die and the new generations will forget'[28]. I keep that symbolic key and raise my voice around the globe in defiance of that. Yes, the old have died, but the new generations still remember, and one day we will go home.

---

28 Izzeldin Abuelaish, 2001, *I Shall Not Hate: A Gaza Doctor's Journey on the Road to Peace and Human Dignity,* Bloomsbury Publishing, London, p. 35.

RETURN TO TARSHIHA

In 2015 my oldest son, Chaker Khazaal, made the journey I cannot. He returned to Tarshiha, not as a Palestinian, but as a Canadian. He became the first member of our family to walk on the streets of our ancestors since they were cast out in October 1948.

In 2002, my grandfather passed away. On his deathbed Tarshiha was all he talked about. He had lived his entire life dreaming of the day he would return, and when fate betrayed him, dreaming became all that he had. He even asked to be buried there—a final wish that was impossible to grant. No Palestinian refugees are permitted to travel into Israel or any of the Palestinian territories. Tarshiha is only 100 kilometres away from the Lebanese capital of Beirut, but with a closed border standing between Lebanon and Israel, Tarshiha is practically unreachable.

Sixty-seven years after his exodus, I embarked on a journey to find Tarshiha, the place my grandfather called home. As a Canadian citizen now, I have become the first member of my family able to legally enter Israel.

As I drove north from Jerusalem, my mind was filled with memories of my grandfather. I thought of all the stories he had told of

191

Tarshiha—about the mosque, the church, and the roads with the olive trees. I listened to the music my grandfather loved and lost myself in the reverie. I was scared and excited at the same time. I was finally about to see the land my grandfather had painted in my imagination for so many years.

When I first came upon a sign that read Tarshiha, I stopped, took a photo with it ... and cried. I wasn't sure what to do next. Surrounded by strangers, I didn't know where to begin my journey to my family's origins. Suddenly I was living my grandfather's dream, seeing Tarshiha with my own eyes. The old streets are exactly as he had described them. The mosque is there, the church still stood. I had the biggest smile on my face, mixed with fears and tears. I stopped a young man walking down the street. 'Is this Tarshiha?' I asked. He answered in Arabic, 'Yes, this is Tarshiha'.

I knew it was, but I sought spoken affirmation, nonetheless. Finally, I could hear someone telling me I was in my home village. The young man stared at me and saw a lost boy with watery eyes. But he could not fully see the storm of emotions hitting me at the moment.

'My grandfather lived here over 60 years ago. His name is Ragheb Kiblawi; his father's name is Saleh Kiblawi.'

'Sorry, I don't know who that is,' he told me.

He stopped a car passing by, and the driver said the same. I was less than surprised, as they both appeared much too young to have known my grandfather. I left just a little disappointed. I found a falafel shop while searching for a place to eat and collect myself. Some of the town's residents were gathered inside. When the shop owner heard my story, he became excited. Finally, I wasn't the only one! The shop owner asked someone to take me to an old man well-versed in the history of Tarshiha. I was led inside a tiny hut, where he sat surrounded by maps. He was a real estate agent, and he welcomed me warmly.

I told him who I was, and he immediately recalled my family.

'Saleh owned a cafe, I remember.'

I let out a sigh of relief at the further affirmation of my grand-father's stories. They weren't just stories, but a reality. The old man asked someone to take me to where my grandfather once lived. When we arrived, I requested my companion to give me some time alone, to which he complied. There, life's countless possibilities flashed through every space of my consciousness. I was imagining the life for our family had there been no war, and no displacement.

I took a video of the neighbourhood so that I could share it with my family still living as Palestinian refugees in Lebanon. For them, it is even more emotional. It is the place they are forbidden to visit, but now they could see it through my eyes.

I walked the streets of Tarshiha for a long time. I listened to stories from any resident who would tell me one. I found an old man who knew my grandfather, and he told me tales that reminded me of him. My grandfather's stories were real, the village is real, and experiencing them for myself will help keep those memories alive.

Those around my age living in Tarshiha didn't want me to leave. They longed to hear about the people who left years ago, and they were living their own tales through me.

While I could not fulfil my grandfather's dream of burying him in Tarshiha, I did the best I could. I planted an olive tree for my grandfather in his village. I chose to plant the tree as a symbol of hope and peace for my family and for the remaining inhabitants of Tarshiha, that they may be spared further conflict and war. And that one day my family in exile might, too, be able to return to Tarshiha.[29]

---

29 An account of Chaker's visit was originally published in 2015 in the *HuffPost*, 'A Refugee Returns Home: The Journey to My Roots'.